Come Boldly to the Throne

SANCTUARY THEMES IN HEBREWS

Ekkehardt Mueller

Pacific Press® Publishing Association
Nampa, Idaho
Oshawa, Ontario, Canada
www.pacificpress.com

Design by Dennis Ferree
Cover illustration by Justinen Creative Group

Additional copies of this book may be purchased at
http://www.adventistbookcenter.com

All Scripture quotations are from the Revised Standard Version
unless otherwise noted.

Library of Congress Cataloging-in-Publication Data

Mueller, Ekkehardt, 1950-
Come boldly to the throne : sanctuary themes in Hebrews / Ekkehardt Mueller.
p. cm.
Includes bibliographical references.
ISBN: 0-8163-1974-X
1. Bible. N.T. Hebrews—Criticism, interpretation, etc. I. Title.

BS2775.52.M84 2003
227'.8706—dc21 2002193026

03 04 05 06 07 • 5 4 3 2 1

Table of Contents

Table of Contents

Introduction

Bookstores can be quite fascinating, especially the larger ones that carry a great variety of books. Oftentimes we enjoy browsing through these different works. Some are quite easy to read. Others may be more demanding. Some books we can read through in one sitting. Others are quite heavy and technical, and we may have to reread sentences to understand them. But interestingly enough, it is oftentimes the "heavier" books that benefit us most.

The Gospels of the New Testament and the book of Acts belong to the type of literature that is more easily accessible. The book of Hebrews belongs to the New Testament writings that are on the heavier side. We need both—books that inspire us and that we cannot stop reading and books that we have to digest thoroughly to grasp their meaning.

The author of Hebrews himself distinguished between milk and solid food (see Heb. 5:12), and in chapter 6:1 he encouraged his readers to "leave the elementary doctrines of Christ and go on to maturity." In writing the book of Hebrews, he had a threefold purpose in mind: to help those who might be tempted to fall away from the Christian faith, to expand our knowledge of Jesus' ministry, and to help us to focus on our Lord. Hebrews strongly emphasizes the centrality of Jesus Christ and tells us: Do not give up when questions haunt you and when it gets tough!

Let us accept this challenge and see how the Epistle to the Hebrews not only addresses the original audience but confronts, comforts, and enlightens us today.

Jesus and the Book of Hebrews

When we receive a letter, normally we want to know who sent it. That's true of the letters and books of the New Testament too. While we realize that God was the ultimate Author, knowing the identity of the human author and of the recipients and the approximate date of writing may help us to understand the original situation and therefore the text itself. It also allows us to apply the text correctly to our modern circumstances.

The Epistle to the Hebrews differs from other New Testament letters in that it doesn't contain an introduction telling us who wrote the letter and to whom it was addressed. Therefore, we have to find hints about the author and readership in the letter itself.

I. Who Sent It?

Traditionally, this letter was considered to belong among the Pauline writings. Older Bible versions still include the heading "The Epistle of Paul the Apostle to the Hebrews." Today, however, the vast majority of scholars believe that Paul could not have been the author of this New Testament book. Why? (1) Whereas Paul introduces himself by name in all the letters attributed to him, he doesn't in the letter to the Hebrews. (2) The Greek in which Hebrews was written differs from that of the Pauline writings. (3) The theological content of Hebrews differs markedly from the theology of Paul's letters. (4) The Old Testament quotations in Hebrews follow the Septuagint word for word, whereas Paul used some freedom in quoting in the letters that are clearly his.

People have proposed a number of individuals as possible authors of the letter: Clement of Rome, Barnabas, Silas, Stephen, Priscilla, Apollos, and Mary, the mother of Jesus. None of these suggestions is really convincing. Origen (A.D. 185-253) believed that the thoughts in Hebrews originated with Paul, but as to the actual author, he said, "Who wrote the epistle, in truth God knows."[1]

However, there are also arguments supporting Paul's authorship of Hebrews: In the earliest preserved New Testament text that contains this epistle, the P^{46} manuscript of the third century A.D., it is placed among Paul's writings, directly after Romans. Clement of Alexandria (A.D. 150-215) and the Eastern Church were convinced that Paul was the author. Clement suggested that Paul wrote his letter in Hebrew and then Luke translated it into Greek. With regard to the content, it must be kept in mind that a special situation or a specific group of people may require an author to use an approach different from the one he has taken before, so his style of writing may differ from that of his previous works.

We do know that the author must have been a Jew and must have been well educated and well versed in the Old Testament. While the style of writing and the vocabulary do not point to Paul, we know that Paul made use of secretaries (see Rom. 16:22; 2 Thess. 3:17). Such a person may have had some liberty to formulate the thoughts and words of the letter. Only a few church leaders lived before A.D. 70, and they're quite well known. Among them, Paul is the most likely to have written a document as profound as the Epistle to the Hebrews.

The last verses of Hebrews (13:22-25) strongly remind us of the Pauline letters. Ten of those letters mention Timothy, as does this passage (verse 23). The desire to see the recipients of the letter noted here resembles that of Romans 1:11 and Philippians 1:25; 2:24. The wish that grace be with the hearers and readers of the message is a typical Pauline phrase.

So, either of two scenarios—Paul writing in Hebrew and then being translated or his making extensive use of a secretary—answer most of the objections that have been raised to Pauline authorship. E. G. White did not specifically discuss the question of the authorship of Hebrews, but she apparently believed that Paul wrote this letter.[2]

Perhaps, then, Paul wrote Hebrews after all.

II. To Whom?

To whom was the letter addressed? Knowing the intended audience helps us to identify—and understand—the main point of the letter. The focus on the sanctuary system, the priesthood, and related topics, which assumed knowledge of the Old Testament, makes it plausible that the recipients were mainly Jewish Christians. Obviously, these believers were in danger of directly or indirectly abandoning Jesus.

It has been suggested that the people to whom Paul wrote Hebrews were particularly concerned about sins committed after baptism. How could they get rid of those sins? The old system of sacrifices and priestly service had provided a solution. But what could Christians do? Baptism represented cleansing, but what about sins committed after baptism?

Not knowing the answer, Jewish Christians may have been tempted to return to the old system, which at least offered something. "They must be persuaded that, though the sacrifice of Jesus is unrepeatable, it continues to be effective to cope with their present consciousness of sin."[3] Hebrews portrays Jesus as the real sacrifice and the priest who takes care of all sins, past and present.

III. When?

When was Hebrews written? A number of facts suggest it was written before A.D. 70. The ancient Christian document 1 Clement, which was probably written around A.D. 96, quotes the book of Hebrews, so

Hebrews must have been written before this date. Hebrews 13:23 indicates that Timothy, the faithful companion of Paul, was still living at the time the letter was written.

Furthermore, the letter gives the impression that the Jewish sacrificial system was still functioning. People could turn away from Jesus and return to offering bulls and goats. So, the temple in Jerusalem and its services must still have been intact—which indicates a date even prior to A.D. 70, the year the Romans destroyed the temple. Up to then, many Jewish Christians may still have celebrated the Israelite feasts, offered sacrifices, and may have been zealous for the ceremonial laws. They needed to be prepared for the destruction of the Jerusalem temple. They needed an anchor firmer than an earthly building and its ceremonies. They needed to focus on Jesus and His ministry for them in the heavenly sanctuary.[4]

IV. About What?

Hebrews focuses on Jesus. At its very beginning it says that in these last days God has spoken to us through Jesus Christ, His Son and our Lord. He is the Creator and Sustainer, the Savior and the Majesty of the cosmos seated at the right hand of His Father, the representation of God, and God Himself. With Jesus a new eon has come—actually, the end time has begun, though this period encompasses a shorter, intensified end time that immediately precedes the second coming of Jesus.

Hebrews 1 focuses strongly on the exalted position of Jesus and His superiority over the angels. Chapter 2 adds another dimension: Christ's humility. He became one of us, was not afraid to call us His brothers, and, in dying on the cross as the substitutionary sacrifice, has provided salvation and cleansing for us. He understands us and helps us. The end of this chapter introduces Christ's priesthood, which is dependent on His humiliation.

In chapters 3 and 4, after comparing Jesus and Moses, the author develops the topic *rest.* Israel couldn't enter the rest provided by God because of unbelief and disobedience. Today we are challenged not to harden our hearts. The rest that we are able to enter here and now seems to be spiritual rest through salvation in Christ. We participate in this rest through faith in Him. This rest also points to the Sabbathlike eschatological rest that is still to come. The Sabbath, which serves as a sign of creation and salvation, foreshadows this rest. Hebrews 4 ends with the promise that we have access to the throne of grace and may therefore be confident. We have a High Priest.

Chapter 5 compares the earthly high priests with Jesus, our High Priest. The ends of chapters 5 and 6 form an extended warning. The author criticizes the readers for still depending on spiritual "milk"; he calls them not to fall away but to lay "hold of the hope set before us" (6:18). The conclusion of chapter 6 points to the strong comfort, the anchor of our soul, that reaches even into the sanctuary.

In Hebrews 7, Paul shows that Jesus is a high priest like Melchizedek. This priesthood is superior to the Levitical priesthood, in which Jesus—born of the tribe of Judah—could never take part. The last section of this chapter particularly emphasizes the character of Jesus' high-priestly ministry and its results.

Hebrews 8–10a comprise the climax of the book. Chapter 8 stresses the importance of the new covenant, and chapter 9 contrasts the heavenly sanctuary and Jesus' sacrifice with the old tabernacle and its service. The new covenant allows Jesus to be our High Priest. It surpasses the old covenant, for instance, through placing the law in the heart of believers. And chapter 9 and the first part of chapter 10 proclaim that only the sacrifice of Jesus can atone for sins. This sacrifice is unique, unrepeatable, and sufficient. Because Jesus died, sins can now be forgiven.

The second part of Hebrews 10 repeats—this time at greater length—the warning about judgment. The call not to throw away one's confidence is answered by the last verse of the chapter: "We are not of those who shrink back." Hebrews 11, then, follows with the famous section about those who did not fall away—the heroes of faith.

Chapter 12 declares that, because we have the cloud of witnesses pictured in chapter 11, we fix our eyes upon Jesus. Christians are on their way to the heavenly Zion. In faith they have already arrived there (12:22), and yet, "we are seeking the city which is to come" (13:14). While the last two chapters of the epistle contain admonitions to live a Christian life and a number of promises, they also point to Jesus, who shed His blood for us and who suffered outside the gate.

Hebrews contains large blocks of warning and admonition (2:1-4; 3:7–4:13; 5:11–6:8; 10:26-39; 12:1-29; and 13:1-17) next to blocks of theological exposition. These blocks alternate. George Rice has suggested the following helpful outline:[5]

Introduction: 1:1-4

I. 1:5–2:4
   Theological Exposé: 1:5-14
   Warning: 2:1
   Judgment: 2:2-4

II. 2:5–4:13
   Theological Exposé: 2:5–3:6
   Warning: 3:7-19
   Judgment: 4:1-13

III. 4:14–6:8
   Theological Exposé: 4:14–5:10
   Warning: 5:11–6:6
   Judgment: 6:7, 8

IV. 6:9–10:39
   Theological Exposé: 6:9–10:25
   Warning: 10:26, 27
   Judgment: 10:28-31
   Secondary Warning and Judgment: 10:32-39

V. 11:1–12:29
   Theological Exposé: 11:1-40
   Warning: 12:1-24
   Judgment: 12:25-29
   Pastoral Exhortation: 13:1-19

Conclusion: 13:20-25

These warnings and admonitions reveal to us what was at stake when the Epistle to the Hebrews was written. The recipients were being tempted to reject or lose salvation, to drift away from sound proclamation and NT teaching, to miss the divine rest because of disobedience, to become weary and sin willfully, and to live an unethical life.

The structure of Hebrews shows us that theology/doctrine and life go together and should not be separated. On one hand, theology without application to the everyday life of the believer may become irrelevant. On the other, focusing solely on relevance and application and neglecting the backbone of sound biblical teaching may lead to mere enthusiasm and sentimentalism. Biblical doctrines rightly understood will always affect our practical life, and practice and lifestyle must always be informed by Scripture. Otherwise we end up in pure pragmatism and situation ethics, in which biblical principles no longer play any role and in which the distinction between right and wrong disappears because people judge to be correct whatever serves them best.

Today, some of us assign theology and biblical studies to the specialists and rid ourselves of the responsibility—the challenge, but also the joy—of a deep study of the Word of God.[6] This threatens our Christian experience with shallowness. Others are more inclined to scientific research, but may superimpose the theories of sociology, psychology, and the natural sciences upon Scripture. In too many churches all but a minority of the members consider doctrines and theological studies irrelevant, outdated, and boring.

> The apostle, aware of the spiritual problems of his hearers, has thought through carefully to a solution. They have failed to grow and still are ready only for milk—*but milk will not help them any longer.* Their situation is serious. If they are to be saved from the perils of neglect or rejection, they must take solid food. . . . His emphasis upon intellectual activity is unique among the writings of the New Testament. The apostle declares that theology—even difficult theology—aids Christian growth.

> In at least some cases of stagnation, the *only hope* will come through the solid food of theology.[7]

This is a lesson that we need to learn. Serious Bible study can help us to grow spiritually. Spiritual "milk" is not sufficient in the long run.

V. Why Was It Written?

Although we have already hinted at the concern that led Paul to write the Epistle to the Hebrews, we will summarize briefly here: This epistle says that those who have backslidden after having tasted the heavenly gift and after having received the Holy Spirit cannot renew their repentance since they crucify the Son of God a second time (6:4-6). Apparently, Paul's audience, especially those with a Hebrew background, may have been tempted to fall away from the Lord.

Nevertheless, the perspective of the book is very positive. Jesus' sacrifice is once for all and is sufficient for all who are willing to accept it. We have a high priest in heavenly places, access to God, and absolute confidence. Hebrews 10:22, 23, together with the parallel statements in 4:14-16, may present the theme of the epistle: Do not give up on Jesus! The best has come. Jesus is the fulfillment of the Old Testament types and the guarantee of salvation.

This is an important message even for us today. Jesus has died for us. The Cross is the turning point of history and of our fate. Jesus serves as our high priest, intervening on our behalf. Therefore, we have confidence. Therefore, we are called to draw close to God and receive mercy, grace, and help. The way to the heavenly sanctuary, the way to the throne of God, is open! God is our Father, and we are His children, and He treats us as such (Heb. 12:7-9). We are washed and rid of a bad conscience. Our sins are forgiven, and we need not worry about them anymore. Jesus has saved His children. And we in turn are challenged to hold fast to our confession. We are called never to let go of this Jesus.[8]

VI. Jesus in Hebrews

1. In the Introduction to Hebrews (1:1-4)

Hebrews has a unique introduction. Verses 1 and 2a are to some degree parallel, yet they form a contrast. They claim that God has revealed Himself in special ways. There is a general revelation of God—i.e., through nature—and a specific revelation of God—through His messengers. Hebrews is concerned with only the latter. The fact is that God is not a hidden god to whom we have no access. He has spoken in the past, and He has spoken in these last days in which the audience of Hebrews lives. The incarnation, life, death, resurrection, and ascension of Jesus form the great turning point of history; these events brought about a radical change. They marked the beginning of the last days; now we wait for Jesus to return.

God's Revelation

	Verse 1	*Verse 2a*
How?	In many portions and in many ways—	
When?	long ago	in these last days
Who?	He spoke[God]	has spoken
To whom?	to the fathers	to us
Through whom?	the prophets	His Son

The present revelation in Jesus Christ surpasses all the revelations through the prophets. The hearers and readers of Hebrews live in this privileged time of God's supreme revelation. "The consummation of the revelatory process, the definitive revelation, took place when He who was not one of the 'goodly fellowship of the prophets' but the very Son of God came."[9]

Paul's introductory statement sets the stage for the main message of the letter. If Jesus is God's highest revelation, how can we return to the old covenant, rejecting what God has granted us in Jesus?

The second part of the introduction shows us who this Son is, giving a sevenfold description of Him. Again an outline, which closely follows the original text, may help us to grasp the meaning.

The Son in Hebrews 1:2b-4

1. Whom He has appointed heir of all things
2. Through whom He created the universe
3. Who
   - being the radiance of his glory and the exact likeness of his being
   - sustaining all things by the word of his power
   - having made purification of the sins sat down at the right hand of the majesty on high
   - having become as much superior to the angels as he has inherited a more excellent name than they.

This passage makes three major statements about Jesus: (1) He is the appointed Heir of all things—a title that stresses His dignity "to the highest place in heaven."[10] (2) He is the Creator. (3) He sat down on the throne at the Father's right side, the place of highest honor.

Why does He have such an exalted position? The bulleted phrases answer this question. Jesus is the King on the right hand of the Father because: (a) He is the radiance of the Father's glory and the exact representation of the Father, i.e., He shares God's divinity. (b) He is the One who sustains everything and leads it toward its intended goal. And (c) He, as the Savior, has brought purification of sins. Verse 4 further describes His exalted position: He is superior to the angels and has inherited a more excellent name than theirs.

The third statement, which pictures Jesus sitting at the right hand of God, portrays Him after His ascension and enthronement as the Priest-King of the universe. The phrase "having sat down at the right hand of the Majesty on high" alludes to Psalm 110. This psalm portrays the Messiah as the Priest-King, and Paul develops this concept. In chapter 1 he introduces Jesus to us as the King, superior to the angels. In chapter 2 he adds the priestly function, which he develops more fully in the rest of the letter.

The issue of "purification of sins" mentioned in these first verses of Hebrews belongs to the heart of the letter. It is because of sin that Jesus became our Brother, offered Himself as a sacrifice, and serves as our High Priest. Thus, the introduction contains in a nutshell the most important themes of Hebrews.

2. In the Body of the Letter

Hebrews uses a great number of titles and names to describe its Hero: (1) Jesus (2:9), (2) Christ (3:14), (3) Jesus Christ (10:10), (4) Son (1:5), (5) Son of Man (2:6), (6) Son of God (6:6), (7) the Firstborn (1:6), (8) God (1:8-9), (9) Lord (1:10), (10) Priest (5:6), (11) High Priest (2:17), (12) Great High Priest (4:14), (13) Apostle (3:1), (14) Forerunner (6:20), (15) the Pioneer of their salvation (2:10, RSV), (16) the Source of eternal salvation (5:9), (17) the Guarantee of a better covenant (7:22), (18) the Mediator of a new covenant (9:15), (19) the Pioneer and Perfecter of our faith (12:2, RSV), and (20) the great Shepherd of the sheep (13:20).

An extremely positive picture emerges. Although Jesus is God, He cares about us. He has secured our salvation. He serves as our mediator. He will bring us to the ultimate goal.

Conclusion

Jesus is the only hope for humanity and for the church. Therefore, the apostle paints a magnificent picture of who Jesus is and what He does to save us. Knowing Jesus in His multifaceted ministry will protect us from falling away, maintaining our confidence in and our hold on Him.

Hebrews invites us to turn our eyes from the earthly sanctuary to the heavenly reality. It says that the old covenant finds its fulfillment in Jesus and the new covenant and that the earthly tabernacle has been replaced by the reality of the heavenly. It tells us that Jesus is the true Sacrifice and High Priest. Because He has saved us, we follow Him. We do not give up on Him. As pilgrims, we are on the way to the city that is to come, where we will see Him face to face.

1. Quoted by Eusebius, *Ecclesiastical History,* vi. 25. 14

2. See, e.g., Ellen G. White, *The Great Controversy* (Nampa, Idaho: Pacific Press Publishing Association, 1950), 347.

3. B. Lindars, *The Theology of the Letter to the Hebrews* (Cambridge: Cambridge University Press, 1994), 59.

4. Cp. *Seventh-day Adventist Bible Commentary,* F. D. Nichol, ed. (Hagerstown, Md.: 1957), 7:389.

5. George E. Rice, "Apostasy as a Motif and Its Effect on the Structure of Hebrews," *Andrews University Seminary Studies,* 23 (1985), 29–35.

6. Cp. Fritz Guy, *Thinking Theologically: Adventist Christianity and the Interpretation of Faith* (Berrien Springs: Andrews University Press, 1999), 165, 166.

7. William G. Johnsson, *In Absolute Confidence* (Nashville: Southern Publishing Association, 1979), 22.

8. See especially Ellen G. White, *The Ministry of Healing* (Nampa, Idaho: Pacific Press Publishing Association, 1942), 167.

9. Leon Morris, *Hebrews,* F. E. Gaebelein, ed., *The Expositor's Bible Commentary* (Grand Rapids: Zondervan Publishing House, 1981), 12:13.

10. Morris, 13.

CHAPTER 2

Jesus, Our King

Kings have always intrigued both children and adults. They're featured in fairy tales and films, and some are around even today. History tells us that some were benevolent rulers. Others were cruel, possessed by the desire to extend their influence, to subdue other nations, or to create world empires.

The Bible presents God as a king—an excellent king, fair and just, loving and caring for the citizens of His kingdom. Jesus is even called the King of kings (Rev. 17:14; 19:16). In Hebrews, Jesus, the Priest-King, is even more than a benevolent ruler. He saves His children and personally cares for them. He can do that because He has received all authority in heaven and earth.

I. Jesus the King

Hebrews names as kings the pharaoh of the time of Moses (11:23, 27) and Melchizedek (7:1, 2). Interestingly, while it never calls Jesus "king," it portrays Him in this role.

He sits at God's right hand (1:3, 13; 8:1; 10:12; 12:2). After having offered Himself as a sacrifice, Jesus took His seat at God's right hand. This phrase points to the enthronement and subsequent kingship of the Messiah. Whereas angels stand around the throne of God, the Son is depicted as sitting. "At no time are angels ever conceived of as sitting, and therefore the enthronement of Jesus at once establishes his superiority. Not only is his sovereignty stated, but also his absolute power over his enemies."[1]

The right side is the side of honor. When King Solomon wanted to honor his mother, he ordered a throne to be brought in and placed at his right side on which she would take a seat (see 1 Kings 2:19). The enthronement of Jesus at the right hand of the Majesty of heaven conveys His supreme exaltation and His incomparable grandeur. The phrase is taken from Psalm 110, which is the only Old Testament reference to someone being "enthroned beside God."[2] The Son is very closely associated with the Father and shares in His rule and glory.

He has a throne (1:8). The term *throne* occurs four times in Hebrews. In chapter 1:8 it refers to the throne of Christ. In chapter 8:1; 12:2; and probably also in 4:16 it refers to the throne of God the Father.

Hebrews 1:8 applies a quotation from Psalm 45:6 to Jesus. He's the only Person aside from God the Father who this letter says has a throne. This verse teaches Jesus' divinity. In verses 5-7 Paul introduces the angels, none of whom he calls "Son" and all of whom, he says, worship Jesus and are servants. Then he makes a sharp contrast: "Of the angels he says: . . . but of the Son *he says:* Your throne, O God, [stands] forever and ever" (Heb. 1:7, 8, NRSV). Verse 8 stresses Jesus' eternal rule as the divine king.

He has a scepter (1:8). The term *scepter* is used not only in Psalm 45:6, which is quoted in Hebrews 1:8, but also in Psalm 110:2 and Psalm 2:9.[3] All these are Messianic psalms and royal psalms. Paul combines these different Old Testament references to the Messiah to show that Jesus is the rightful King.

He has a kingdom (1:8). Besides the kingdoms of the world (Heb. 11:33), there is also the kingdom of Christ (Heb. 1:8). Because Christ's kingdom is a reality, the saints can receive "a kingdom that cannot be shaken" (Heb. 12:28).

His enemies are made a footstool for His feet (1:13; 10:13). Footstools of kings—as, for instance, the footstool to the throne of Tutankhamen in Egypt—have been found with pictures of captive enemies painted or carved on the sides.[4] The phrase "making the enemies a footstool" tells us that Jesus is the King and that all His enemies will be defeated and have to bow before Him.

He is crowned with glory and honor and all things are subject to Him (2:7-9). In Hebrews 2, Paul focuses on Christ's humiliation, which led to His exaltation. In this case he uses Psalm 8 rather than one of the royal psalms. The phrase "subjecting all things under his feet" recalls the previous statement that the enemies are made a footstool for His feet, thus linking Psalm 8:6 to Psalm 110:1. Again, the kingship motif seems to be present.

He is compared to Melchizedek, the king of Salem (5:6, 10; 6:20; 7:1-22). Finally, Jesus is presented as the antitype of Melchizedek. This Old Testament figure was not only a priest, he was also a king. However, Jesus far excels him both as the king of peace and well-being and as the king of righteousness.

So, Hebrews clearly portrays Jesus as the king of the universe. Although this kingship motif is found throughout Hebrews, chapter one contains its clearest portrayal.

II. Jesus the Promised Priest-King

Hebrews is unique in portraying Jesus as a *priest*-king.

1. The Old Testament Quotations in Hebrews 1

Hebrews 1:4-14 praises Jesus in increasingly exalted terms: (1) Jesus is the Son (vs. 5), the Messianic King. (2) Jesus is to be worshiped (vs. 6). (3) Jesus is King and God from eternity to eternity (vss. 8, 9). (4) Jesus is Creator and is Yahweh (vss. 10-12). And (5) Jesus participates in God's rule, and all will be subject to Him, the real King (vs. 13).

Thompson has suggested the following helpful outline of Hebrews 1:[5]

Hebrews 1:3-13

Vs. 3	Psalm 110:1	
	Vss. 5, 6	Two quotations on the Son
		One quotation on the angels
	Vss. 7-12	One quotation on the angels
		Two quotations on the Son
Vs. 13	Psalm 110:1	

The kingship motif in Hebrews is based on a number of Old Testament passages. They include Psalms 2, 45, and 110—all of them being so-called royal psalms. The most prominent text is Psalm 110. This psalm is used throughout the book of Hebrews, whereas the other quotations are limited to the first chapter only. Psalm 110 also provides the backbone of Hebrews 1. No wonder it has been suggested that the entire letter of Hebrews could be considered a sermon based on this particular passage. The heavy emphasis on Old Testament passages tells us not only that the Old and the New Testaments belong together but also that the Old Testament prophecies about the future King-Messiah find their fulfillment in Jesus and in Him only.

In Psalm 110 the Lord addresses David's Lord, who is the Messiah. Verse one of this psalm mentions the enthronement of the King-Messiah and verse 4 the bestowal of the priesthood on Him. Other verses talk about the world dominion of this King and say that He will share in Yahweh's reign.

In Matthew 22:41-46,[6] Jesus quotes Psalm 110:1 and asks the Pharisees how the Messiah could be David's Son when David calls Him his Lord. Obviously, Jesus was telling the Pharisees that the Messiah is not only David's Son but the divine King, and that Psalm 110, which they interpreted messianically,[7] refers to Him. In Matthew 26:64, Jesus seems to allude to the same passage when He states that the Son of man will be " 'seated at the right hand of Power and coming on the clouds of heaven.' "[8]

According to Mark 16:19, Jesus "was taken up into heaven and took his seat at God's right hand" (NAB). Thus, the Old Testament prophecy was fulfilled in Him. Peter, in his sermon at Pentecost, spoke of the enthronement of Christ " 'at the right hand of God' " (Acts 2:33). In the next two verses he quoted from Psalm 110:1, interpreting that passage as depicting Jesus' exaltation as king after His resurrection and ascension. He said the visible sign on earth of Christ's enthronement in heaven was the gift of the Holy Spirit on Pentecost.[9] Paul also taught that Jesus is at the right hand of God (see Rom. 8:34; Eph. 1:20; Col. 3:1) and that "he must reign until he has put all his enemies under his feet" (1 Cor. 15:25). Hebrews 1:3, 13; 8:1; 10:12 also refer to Psalm 110:1.

2. Christ's Unique Kingship in Hebrews

Hebrews is unique in that it portrays Jesus not only as a king but as the king who is also a priest forever. Some Jewish circles expected a royal Messiah from the tribe of Judah and a priestly Messiah from the tribe of Levi. Hebrews unites the offices of the royal Messiah and the priestly Messiah. It indicates that the royal psalms are fulfilled in Jesus, the Priest-King. His reign has already begun, but it also has a future dimension: the subjection of all His enemies at His return.

During the kingly period of Israel's history the offices of king and priest were always kept separate. Only in the intertestamental period do we find a priest-king in Judaism. The Maccabean ruler Aristobulus I (104 B.C.) claimed royalty in addition to the priestly office, and some of those who followed him on the throne also ruled as priest-kings. But these kings were not Davidic kings. They were descendants of Aaron and Levi and thus not a fulfillment of Old Testament prophecies. In addition, they were corrupt and sometimes cruel, and no example of an ideal priest-king.

Only Jesus fulfills the prophesied role of priest-king. When Joseph named Mary's baby "Jesus," he adopted the child as his own son. Consequently, Jesus was incorporated into Joseph's genealogy, which traces back through the line of Davidic rulers to David himself (see Matthew 1). But how could Jesus be a priest when those holding this role must be able to trace their ancestry through Aaron to Levi?[10] Hebrews says this priest-king was not to be a Levitical priest, but a priest according to a totally different order, the order of Melchizedek.

III. Time and Place of Jesus' Kingship

The author of Hebrews doesn't discuss the nature and extent of the Son's kingly rule prior to His incarnation. He affirms that Jesus existed prior to Creation and ascribes eternal preexistence to Him. But what Paul considered important was the realization that Christ's reign began after His death, resurrection, and ascension to heaven, when He sat down at the right hand of God after "he had made purification for sins" (1:3). His humiliation through incarnation and death was followed by His resurrection and exaltation (2:6-9). The cross was followed by the crown (12:2).

Hebrews contains, at least indirectly, the following chronology: (1) Jesus' preexistence, (2) His incarnation, (3) His enthronement, (4) "today," and (5) the final victory. It is the "today" (3:7) that the letter to the Hebrews focuses on. "Today" the readers have to make their decision. "Today" they have to cling to that Person named Jesus, who is the most powerful King and the most compassionate High Priest.

God's throne is connected to His heavenly sanctuary (8:1, 2),[11] and Jesus has taken His seat at God's right hand. He rules the universe, including our world. Standing before Pilate He could say, " 'My kingship is not of this world' " (John 18:36). Were it a kingship of this world, it would be limited in time and space, but Jesus is King without restrictions. The extent of His kingship tells us much about His power and authority, His omnipotence and wisdom. In part, He rules to sustain creation (1:3). Without Him the created order would collapse. He is the One who cares for our well-being and especially for our salvation.

IV. Character, Attributes, and Work of Jesus the King

What kind of king is Jesus?

He is the King of peace and salvation (Heb. 7:2; 2:3). Like Melchizedek, Jesus is the King of peace. The name "Salem" is connected to the Hebrew concept of *shalom.* It suggests peace, completeness, and welfare. Its nuances include good health, prosperous relations to others, friendship, and even the idea of salvation. Jesus is the Peacemaker par excellence. But the Greek term *salvation* is also used to describe His work and the goal of His life: "He is able to save forever those who draw near to God through Him" (7:25, NASB). He is "the source of eternal salvation for all who obey him" (5:9).

He is the King of righteousness and justice (Heb. 7:2; 1:8). Jesus is just and absolutely fair. He shows no partiality. He is also righteous. God's righteousness puts humans in the right relationship with the Deity. Furthermore, Jesus loves righteousness and hates sin (1:9).

He is the King of self-sacrificial love and kindness (Heb. 1:3; 2:9, 10; 7:1; 12:2-6). In Jesus there is no selfishness or egocentrism. He lives for others and He loves us. He was willing to suffer and die because He wanted to save us from eternal death. He is willing to bless because He cares for our well-being. He is not only our Savior but also our Example (12:2, 3).

He is the King of humility and servant-leadership (Heb. 2:11; 8:2). Jesus is sovereign Lord of the universe; nevertheless, He calls us brothers and sisters.

He is the caring King (Heb. 12:2, 3; 2:11). Jesus is the "author and perfecter of our faith" (12:2, NKJV). Believers need not rely on themselves and their own so-called merits. They can cultivate an intimate relationship with Christ. This King has the power to initiate faith and to transform His saints.

He is the Priest-King (Heb. 7:25). Jesus intercedes for those who turn to Him. "We are not to think of Jesus as an orante standing ever before the Father with outstretched arms, like the figures in the mosaics of the catacombs, and with strong crying and tears pleading our cause in the presence of a reluctant God; but as a throned Priest-King, asking what He will from a Father who always hears and grants His requests."[12] Jesus helps us (2:16; 4:16). This help may consist of spiritual, physical, psychical, and also material aid.

He is the immutable King (Heb. 1:12; 13:8). This concept does not mean that Jesus is unaffected by our joys, sorrows, and decisions. It means that His love, kindness, and justice never change, never fail. We can rely upon Him always. He will carry out His plan of salvation, bring to an end this evil age (1:12), and take His children to the heavenly homeland and His glorious city (11:16; 13:14).

V. Jesus, Our King

What does Jesus' kingship mean in practical terms?

1. The King's Expectations

Nowadays many people consider liberty and accountability irreconcilable. But kingship means authority on the part of the king and subordination on the part of his subjects.

King Jesus does not force us to take a stand for Him and serve Him. He wants us to make free decisions. He loves us and waits for our love. Yet He has certain demands and expectations. As the sovereign Lord, this is His right. Hebrews links some of His expectations to His role as king.

Jesus wants us to be completely committed to Him. He wants us to avoid falling away (6:4-6). He expects diligence and eagerness and earnestness in serving Him and others, in maintaining the hope, and in following the example of the great pioneers of faith and patience (6:10-13).

Jesus wants us to approach God with assurance. The King of the universe is not our buddy; we need to approach Him respectfully. Yet our God is not just the distant God; He is also very close. We must esteem both His transcendence and His immanence. Our relationship to God must maintain the healthy balance of approaching Him as the sovereign Ruler of the universe and as our close Friend.

Furthermore, King Jesus challenges us to hold fast our confession (10:23), to get rid of every sin, to persevere in the Christian race (12:1), and to keep our eyes fixed on Him rather than on ourselves or our problems (12:2). He calls us to "strive for peace with all men, and for the holiness without which no one will see the Lord" (12:14). Holy conduct is dynamic; it must grow. To stand still is to regress. Jesus wants us to become more and more like Himself in character, behavior, and service. When we come to Him, He accepts us as we are. But He wants to transform and sanctify us as we live with Him day by day. He wants us to live joyously because we are saved and because He is our Lord. He wants us to reconfirm our decision to accept Him as our Lord and King and to live our life with Him.

Yet whatever our decision may be, He still remains the Lord and King.

2. The King's Support

While Jesus has expectations of us, they don't comprise all of our relationship with Him. He is ready to help and support us in each moment of our life. Someone has calculated that the people of Israel during their journey through the desert needed approximately 4,500 tons of food and about 13 million gallons of water daily. That's enough food to fill two trains, each a mile long. The food would cost approximately $10 million (U.S.) per day. And God provided food for 14,600 days—the Lord really helps!

As God has cared for His children in the past, so He cares for us today. He is still the same Lord, ready to intervene for our sake, sustaining us each moment of our life. He hears our prayers. He changes difficult circumstances. When we're depressed, He holds our hand. He sends us people who are willing to carry our burdens. He helps us to go on when everything looks bleak and hopeless. Although it may seem that Christians are big losers, in reality they are winners. We will triumph because Jesus has triumphed. Through Him we are victorious.

Conclusion

Although Hebrews never directly calls Jesus "king," the kingship motif permeates the entire letter. His exaltation is the consequence of His humiliation. But Jesus is not simply a king or even the most powerful king. He is the Priest-King, and as such has entered another stage of the plan of salvation. The time will come when absolute peace will be restored again.

Hebrews assures those who live in the time between Jesus' crucifixion and His second coming that we can rely on Him in every respect. In our Priest-King we can find forgiveness, salvation, understanding, help, and strength. Therefore, there is no reason to fall away from the Lord (6:6). We should determine to accept Jesus the King as the Lord of our life and to follow Him wherever He may lead us.

---

1. Donald Guthrie, *The Letter to the Hebrews, Tyndale New Testament Commentaries* (Grand Rapids: Wm. B. Eerdmans Publishing Company, 1993), 78.

2. Cp. William L. Lane, *Hebrews 1-8, Word Biblical Commentary,* (Dallas: Word Books, 1991), 47A:16.

3. Cp. Rev. 12:5; 19:15; 2:27.

4. Cp. Siegfried H. Horn, *Seventh-day Adventist Bible Dictionary* (Washington: Review and Herald Publishing Association, 1979), 385, 386, 1117.

5. J. W. Thompson, "The Structure and Purpose of the Catena in Heb. 1:5-13," *Catholic Biblical Quarterly* 1976, 38 (3):353.

6. See also Mark 12:35-37; Luke 20:41-44.

7. S. Kistemaker, *The Psalm Citations in the Epistle to the Hebrews* (Amsterdam: Wed. G. van Soest N. V., 1961), 27.

8. See also Mark 14:62; Luke 22:69.

9. In Acts 5:30-32, Peter returned to the same topic.

10. In the time of Nehemiah some priests "searched their family records, but their names could not be found written there; hence they were degraded from the priesthood" (Neh. 7:64, NAB).

11. See also Rev. 7:15.

12. H. B. Swete, *The Ascended Christ* (London: Macmillan and Co., 1916), 95.

Jesus: One of Us

At the airport in Tel Aviv, Israel, a young English woman who needed a ride to Jerusalem took a seat next to the driver of one of the shuttles. The driver, however, told her that she was not supposed to sit there and had to find another seat in the van. She tried the next row of seats, where an orthodox Jew had found a place. But he also asked her to move farther back. She ended up in the last row. How humiliating!

This incident resembles a parable that Jesus told about finding a seat at a wedding banquet (Luke 14:7-11). It is bad enough when you have to take the lowest seat because you deserve it. It is worse if you deserve the place of highest honor and find yourself in the lowest seat.

I. Jesus' Humiliation

Whereas Hebrews 1 pictures Jesus as the Son of God, Hebrews 2 portrays Him as the brother of human beings. Whereas chapter 1 points to His unparalleled exaltation, chapter 2 depicts His exceptional humiliation.

The first four verses of Hebrews 2 belong to the previous passage, in which Jesus was contrasted with the angels. The beginning of Hebrews 1 says God *spoke* through the prophets of old and then through Jesus, and the passage ends in 2:1-4 by mentioning the word that the angels *spoke* and the salvation *spoken* of, or proclaimed by, the Lord and confirmed by the apostles. The word of the angels was normative, yet how much more important is the greater revelation through the Son!

Hebrews 2:5 changes the topic to Jesus' remarkable lowliness. Although superiority is an important concept in Hebrews, here a reversal takes place. Jesus, who was superior to the angels, took a position lower than theirs. He did what He advised in the parable, taking, figuratively speaking, the lowest position at the table. The Creator became a creature. He accepted the limits of a three-dimensional world—limits of time, power, wisdom, understanding, and many other things. He allowed Himself to be confronted by all kinds of evil and to be affected by the results of sin, such as degeneration, sickness, and death. The difference between a human being and an ant is smaller than the difference between God and humanity. Both ants and humans are creatures; God is the Creator.

However, becoming human wasn't humiliation enough. Jesus didn't enter human society in the palace of the emperor in Rome, the center of the political world at that time. Nor was He born in the palace of the high priest in Jerusalem, the religious center of the world. Jesus had to share His first shelter with animals. He was among the lowliest of the low. The rejection He experienced began with His birth and brought Him to the Cross.

Hebrews 2:5 compares angels with human beings. Verse 16 contrasts them with the children of Abraham. Between these two poles the lowness of Jesus is shown—but also the help He provides for His "brethren." (See the suggested outline of Hebrews 2 on the next page.)

The kingly motif shows up in the first part of the section, which says that all things will be "subjected" to the once humiliated Jesus[1] and that Christ will be "crowned . . . with glory and honor." However, the shift is clearly discernible. The chapter ends with a reference to Christ as high priest. The kingly motif is supplemented by the priestly, which later becomes dominant in the epistle.

Hebrews 2:5-18		
vs. 5 angels and subjection		theme: subjection of everything to Him because of humiliation
vss. 6-8a	OT quotation	
vss. 8b-9	explanation	
vss. 10-11	explanation	theme: help "for brethren" because of humiliation
vss. 12-13	OT quotations	
vss. 14-18	angels, deliverance, and help	

Chronologically, the humiliation came first and was followed by the exaltation. Obviously, the author of Hebrews wanted to introduce Jesus in His majestic role so that the readers would immediately notice in whom they believe and would be reconfirmed in their faith in Him. Then, having introduced Jesus as the transcendent Lord, he brings Him very close to us. Jesus became one of us.

II. Jesus, the Human Par Excellence

In Hebrews 2:6-9, Paul applies Psalm 8 to Jesus. "Remembered and cared for by the Lord, created a little less than a heavenly being, crowned with glory and honor, human beings had been given the status of creature-sovereign with responsibility for the ordering of the creation for God. . . . That goal had been frustrated by sin and death. . . . The recital and celebration of the divine intention awakened the expectation that all that had been placed under human dominion at the time of the creation would yet be subject to humanity in the world to come."[2]

Verse 6 talks about "man" and the "son of man." These terms are used in a synonymous parallelism:

"What is *man*	that you are mindful	of him,
or the *son of man*	that you care	for him?" (NIV).

"Jesus in a representative sense fulfilled the vocation intended for humankind."[3] He is the real and ideal Man. The psalm is perfectly fulfilled only in Him, a fulfillment the Jews had not anticipated. Jesus Himself referred to Psalm 8 (see Matt. 21:16), as did Paul (see 1 Cor. 15:27). Both envisioned Jesus as the fulfillment of this passage.[4]

Some early Christians, especially those with an orientation toward Gnosticism, had a hard time reconciling Jesus' humanity with His divinity. Some of them claimed that at the Jordan baptism the divine Christ entered the man Jesus and then left Him before He died on the cross. Others maintained that Christ had only a phantom body and was not a real human being.[5] But Paul knew that Jesus was a true man.

Two brief notes on Hebrews 2:5-9: There is a difference between Psalm 8:5, "Thou hast made him little less than God[/a god]," and Hebrews 2:7 (NAB), "You made him for a little while lower than the angels." The original Hebrew term can be understood as either "God" or "the angels." The Septuagint, the Greek translation of the Old Testament from which Paul quoted, reads "angels." Paul compared Jesus with angels. He wrote that for a while Jesus was lower than the angels, but now He is superior to them.

The word *Jesus* occurs for the first time in Hebrews in chapter 2:9. Previously, Paul had employed other names and titles to identify the Savior. In using this precious name, Paul has portrayed Him as being very close to us. The King of the universe is one of us, a man—the divine Man—and we are His brothers.

III. Jesus' Suffering

In the civilized world, humiliation does not often include physical violence and abuse. But Jesus endured severe physical suffering that culminated in a violent, extremely painful, slow, and shameful death. His pain and the terror of sensing the utter separation from the One with whom His life had been united from eternity, surpassed any human suffering. Hebrews 2 stresses the intensity of His suffering: (1) "the suffering of death" (vs. 9a); (2) "by the grace of God he might taste death for everyone" (vs. 9b); (3) He "should make the pioneer of their salvation perfect through suffering" (vs. 10); (4) "through death" (vs. 14); (5) "he himself has suffered and been tempted" (vs. 18).

This strong language is not limited to Hebrews 2. Chapters 5:8; 9:26; and 13:12 refer to suffering and, implicitly, death. According to chapter 12:2, Jesus endured the cross and despised the shame, becoming the Author and Perfecter of our faith. Hebrews tells us that He had to suffer death "for everyone" and that only His death would free us from lifelong bondage. One who died like a criminal became the Savior of the world. For many modern people this is a cruel picture; even some Christians and Adventists shrink away from the biblical concept that Jesus died for our sins and offered Himself as a substitutionary sacrifice. The ancient Jews and Greeks also found it unacceptable (see 1 Cor. 1:18-22). In some circles Jesus is seen almost exclusively as an example, not as the One whose righteousness covers our sinfulness. "Yes," these people admit, "He died, but His death was supposed to shock us into returning to God. It is not the means by which God reconciles us to Himself."

However, we must not abandon either the blood terminology or the biblical understanding that Christ suffered vicariously (see 2 Cor. 5:19-21). As representative of the human race, Jesus "must share in the conditions inseparable from the human condition," namely suffering and death.[6] Yet, in many respects what He experienced is not comparable to what any human has experienced. In the first place, His becoming human and dying fulfilled a requirement that no angel and no other human being could ever fulfill.

Second, Jesus did not die for Himself but "for everyone" (2:9). Therefore, His suffering and death have dimensions that we do not fully comprehend. Seldom are we confronted with the choice to die for others. Never can we reconcile others with God by taking their sins upon ourselves. No human being except Jesus was, is, or ever will be forced to experience total separation from God—the second death. While we all have a choice, Jesus' decision to save humanity left Him no other choice than to go through this excruciating torture. "There is an element in the death of Christ that eludes our experience. His is more than an innocent's miscarriage of justice, far more than a martyr's. When we hear the words of desolation from the cross . . . we sense the dimension of divine mystery. The Son has entered into a horror of forsakenness, of utter aloneness, that we cannot comprehend."[7] Even the results of His death we do not completely understand.

Third, Hebrews 2:9 says that "by the grace of God" Jesus tasted "death for everyone." While God's grace was and is extended to us, it was withdrawn from Jesus. He did not experience God's grace. We see God's grace in that He allowed His Son to die for us. Jesus' suffering will always surpass ours by far.

Hebrews 2 clearly spells out the results of Jesus' suffering and death. They include His exaltation, the defeat of Satan, the surety of our salvation, the identification of Jesus with humanity, His efficacy as our High Priest, and His aid for us here and now.

Hebrews 2:10, 17 contain strange formulations. What do these verses mean when they say that God would make Jesus "perfect through suffering" and that He "had to become like his brothers in every way, that he might be a merciful and faithful high priest before God"?[8] Was Jesus imperfect? Would He, the omniscient Lord, not know how humans think, behave, and feel? Was He not merciful and faithful prior to His incarnation (see Exod. 34:6)?

The perfecting of Jesus points to a learning process, but does not mean that He had to be purified from sin. Suffering, temptation, and perfecting indicate that Jesus was a genuine human being, one with us, and fitted as our high priest. He was perfect as God, perfect as a human being, and through suffering became perfect as Savior.[9] From personal experience He knows what it means to be human, to suffer, and to be tempted, and He can sympathize with us in an unprecedented way. "Had He not been tempted in all points, men would have wondered what He would do if He were really hungry, tired out, sick; what He would do if men should revile Him, curse Him, spit upon Him, scourge Him, and at last hang Him on a cross. Would He still retain His composure and pray for His enemies? . . . If . . . God Himself should appear to forsake Him . . . would He still drink the cup or would He draw back?"[10]

Today, many people value as the highest good whatever provides pleasure; they think the meaning of life consists in enjoying life to the fullest. We may need to gain a new perspective on the role and importance of suffering in the life of the Messiah and also in our own lives.

IV. Jesus, Our Brother

Because of Jesus' humiliation, He regards those who are saved through Him as His brothers (2:11). The term *brothers* appears three times in chapter 2, namely in verses 11, 12, and 17. Obviously, Hebrews 2:10-18, which is the second part of the section on Christ's humiliation, is dominated by the motif: Jesus cares for His brothers. These brothers are also "the children God has given" to Jesus (2:13). They are also called "descendants of Abraham," a term that does not describe the entire human race but only those who exhibit Abraham's faith. Thus this second part focuses mainly on believers.[11]

It is amazing that Jesus, the Creator and King of the universe, is willing to call His creatures—even His fallen creatures—brothers! This term points to an intimate relationship: Jesus and His followers comprise one family. Verse 14 emphasizes that He became a partaker of our flesh and blood, of our nature and experience.[12]

Intimacy with Jesus is a tremendous privilege; however, it also poses certain dangers. We may become disrespectful and consider Him merely our buddy. Yes, Jesus is our Brother, but He is also our Teacher, our Lord, and our God. He is the Shepherd, and we are His sheep. He has called us to be His friends, but we are also His servants. We humans are drawn to extremes. We must work at staying balanced. Let us refrain from viewing Jesus as either the distant Ruler of the universe or our buddy. While we can approach Him as our brother, we must do so in all due respect, because despite the intimacy we enjoy with Him, the distinction between Creator and creature remains.

The term *brother* occurs six more times in this biblical book—all the rest of them referring to the relationship between church members. Because we have become brothers and sisters of Jesus, we are also brothers and sisters to one another—an important concept in this age of individualism. Instead of minding our own business, we need to care for one another. We are called to bridge the chasms that grow between nationalities, people groups, races, genders, and generations. Because Jesus drew close to us, we cannot but draw close to one another.

V. Jesus, Our High Priest

The term *high priest* appears for the first time in Hebrews in chapter 2:17. Here it paves the way for the later discussion on this topic. Whereas it is the exaltation of Jesus that makes Him King of the universe, it is His humiliation that prepares Him for His high-priestly office. Hebrews 2:17, 18 lists the qualifications and functions of the true high priest.

To qualify, Jesus had to undergo temptation. Only two times does Paul mention in Hebrews that Jesus was tempted (2:18; 4:15). The second text stresses what is implied in the first one: namely, that despite all the temptations Jesus faced, He never sinned. "Bishop Westcott in his commentary in Hebrews reminds us that the one who falls never knows the full force of temptation, since he fails before the test ends. So Jesus is the only one who has ever lived who has known the extremity of temptations, for only He stayed 'without sin' throughout. Temptation at length succumbed to Him, not He to it."[13]

Jesus' temptations were not limited or superficial. On the contrary, He faced temptations that we never do. We cannot make bread of stones. We cannot command legions of angels, and we cannot escape our death. No doubt Satan worked much harder to entice Him into sin than he does us, because the stakes were so much higher: the battle between Christ and Satan would determine their destinies. It was Jesus' victory over every temptation that qualified Him to be our High Priest.

Now, Jesus is not concerned with angels but with you and me (2:15). He accomplishes the forgiveness of our sins (2:17), and He comes to our aid when we are tempted (2:18). When sin looks attractive and we are tempted to give in, let us remember what it cost Jesus to save us from sin. Let us determine not to hurt Him by making a wrong decision, and let us turn to Him in prayer in order to be empowered to overcome temptation.

Conclusion

Although repetition serves a good purpose, it may also desensitize. Unfortunately, repeated exposure to Christ's humiliation and suffering may harden us. We may not find His sacrifice moving, but instead take it for granted. And whenever we take a relationship for granted, it tends to cool off and become boring. The fervor and devotion dissipate.

Paul wrote Hebrews 2 to rekindle our love for Jesus. He wanted to challenge us to meditate upon our Lord and His utter humiliation. Jesus has tasted death for us; He became the Pioneer of our salvation, conquered Satan and death, freed us from existential fear, and made atonement for our sins. Now He helps us overcome temptation.

In Hebrews 2, Paul calls to our attention aspects of Jesus' suffering that we may have overlooked. He says there is more to explore than we have seen so far. The better we understand Christ's humiliation, the more we will feel drawn to our Lord—the One who has come close enough to us to call us His brothers and sisters, who has saved us, and who as our High Priest gives us aid.

---

1. Cp. this theme in Heb. 1:13.
2. Lane, *Hebrews 1–8*, 46.
3. Lane, *Hebrews 1–8*, 47.
4. Cp. Guthrie, 84, 85.
5. Cp. John's discussion in 1 John 2; 4.
6. F. F. Bruce, *The Epistle to the Hebrews,* rev. ed., *New International Commentary on the New Testament* (Grand Rapids: Wm. B. Eerdmans Publishing Company, 1990), 74.
7. Johnsson, *In Absolute Confidence*, 59.
8. Cp. Heb. 7:28.
9. Cp. *Seventh-day Adventist Bible Commentary,* 7:405.
10. Ibid.
11. Cp. Paul Ellingworth, *The Epistle to the Hebrews, The New International Greek Testament Commentary* (Grand Rapids: Eerdmans, 1993), 152.
12. See also Matt. 12:48-50.
13. Johnsson, *In Absolute Confidence,* 63.

Jesus: Higher and Better

"More, better, and faster" seems to be the motto of our times. We need more money, more vacation, and more luxury. Advertisements remind us constantly of what we're missing. We expect the economy to grow continually and unemployment to decrease. Cars must burn less gas and make us more comfortable. Computers must have more memory and must work faster. We expect new world records at the Olympic Games and other competitions.

"More, better, and faster" is good in that it challenges us and keeps us goal-oriented and on the move. It demands constant improvements. But this motto may also tie us to the rat race. We are never at home, never satisfied, and cannot rest. And if we do become better or faster, arrogance and pride lurk around the corner.

Hebrews addresses the issue of superiority. It contains many adjectives in the comparative form—words such as "better," "higher," and "more excellent." Yes, it says, there is something better than there was in the past. The good has been surpassed by the better. And this "something" has a name: Jesus. Because of Him, we can enjoy a better relationship with God. Hebrews 6:9 mentions "better things that belong to salvation."

I. Jesus' Superiority

Adjectives and adverbs can come in three forms: positive (the standard form), comparative, and superlative. We say, for instance, "good," "better," and "best," and "widely," "more widely," and "most widely." The letter to the Hebrews uses the comparative form extensively, focusing it, to a large extent, on Jesus. But when Hebrews uses the comparative for Jesus, it does not mean to say that someone can be found who is even better. No created being surpasses Jesus.

Hebrews 1:4 introduces the topic of superiority. It says Jesus is far superior to the angels. Two comparatives appear in this verse: "superior" and "more excellent." Hebrews 3 continues this line of thought by showing that Jesus is not only superior to the angels, He is also superior to Moses. Israel's liberator was a gifted writer, one of the greatest leaders of all time, and one of the most important prophets. He "enjoyed privileges no other man has ever known. . . . Abraham was the father of Israel, but Moses was the founder and lawgiver of the nation. God summoned Moses forth from his resting place (see Jude 9), and later honored him with Elijah on the Mount of Transfiguration (Matt. 17:3, 4). As lawgiver and leader Moses surpassed all men of antiquity."[1] Yet Jesus is "worthy of more glory than Moses" (Heb. 3:3, NASB).

Hebrews 7:7 refers to the incident when Abraham gave his tithe to Melchizedek the king of Salem and Melchizedek blessed Abraham. Paul says that "the lesser [person] is blessed by the greater," (NASB), so Melchizedek is greater than Abraham. And, therefore, the priesthood according to the order of Melchizedek is greater than the priesthood that came through Abraham—that is, the Levitical or Aaronic priesthood. Since Jesus belongs to the priesthood of Melchizedek, He is greater than the regular priests of Israel. He is the true High Priest, "holy, innocent, undefiled, separated from sinners, higher than the heavens" (7:26, NAB).

Although superiority is most often ascribed to Jesus, it is not limited to Him. Superiority is a characteristic of the Godhead and of entities and objects directly related to God the Father and Jesus Christ. God the Father is superior (6:13, 16). God's Word is superior (4:12). The heavenly sanctuary is superior (9:11).

According to Hebrews 9:23 this sanctuary requires for its purification "better sacrifices" than the blood of calves and goats[2]—the Son's unique and once-for-all sacrifice (9:25-28). His "sprinkled blood . . . speaks more eloquently than that of Abel" (12:24, NAB). His sacrifice is the only efficacious sacrifice, making Him the author of our salvation and providing for the cleansing of the heavenly sanctuary.

II. The Reasons for Jesus' Superiority

In Hebrews 1:4; 3:3; 7:7, 26; 9:23; and 12:24 Paul tells us why Christ is considered superior:

1. Hebrews 1; 2

Paul compares Jesus to the angels and concludes that He is superior to them (1:4). Hebrews 1 and 2 gives us two basic reasons:[3] He is superior because of what He is and because of what He has done.

Jesus is superior because He is the Son of God (1:2, 5, 8). He is the Creator of all things (1:2, 10), the reflection of God's glory (1:3), and the Sustainer of life and nature (1:3). And Jesus is superior because He—and no one else—has brought about the purification of sins and has taken a seat at the right hand of God (1:3, 13; cp. 2:7-9). In order to save us, Jesus stepped down lower than the angels (2:7-9), becoming one of us. He laid down His life for us. So, in addition to His divine nature, His extraordinary humiliation has made Him superior. There is no one in the entire universe who can be compared with Him, nobody to match Him or measure up to Him.

Hebrews 1:5–2:18

1:5-14	Jesus' exaltation and His relationship to God: Son of God
2:1-4	Admonition
2:5-18	Jesus' humiliation and His relationship to humanity: our Brother

2. Hebrews 3–5

Jesus "is worthy of more glory than Moses" (3:3, NASB). The last part of chapter 2 introduces Jesus as a merciful and faithful high priest

(2:17). From there on Paul develops the priesthood of Christ.[4] In Hebrews 3:1-6 he tells us what Jesus' faithfulness means (3:2, 5, 6). The following section (3:7–4:13) admonishes us regarding our faith/faithfulness (4:2, 3) and warns against unfaithfulness/unbelief (3:12, 19), encouraging us to enter God's Sabbath rest.[5] Hebrews 4:14–5:10 develops the second aspect of Christ's priesthood found in 2:17, namely, mercy.[6]

Hebrews 3:1–5:10

3:1-6: Jesus, the faithful High Priest—His relation to God
3:7–4:13: Admonition to believe/faith
4:14–5:10: Jesus, the merciful High-Priest—His relation to us

Jesus is superior because He is the genuine High Priest and Apostle (3:1). He is not only a servant but the Son, the Founder and Head of the church (3:3, 5, 6). Jesus is superior because He accepted incarnation, suffering, and death (5:7).[7]

Chapters 3–5 say that Jesus surpasses Moses, Joshua, and Aaron. Moses led the people of old through the wilderness. Jesus leads His people today. Joshua could not give Israel rest, but we may "share in Christ" (3:14) and participate in His rest now and particularly when He returns. Aaron was called to be the Levitical high priest (5:4), but God declared Jesus the High Priest according to a different order (5:10). Moses' and Aaron's offices were combined and fulfilled in the Priest-King who serves in the order of Melchizedek.

Although by His nature Jesus is superior to all created beings, He did not strive for superiority. Pride, self-promotion, and the desire to climb the ladder find no place in Him. Paul links superiority to inferiority. However, it is not inferiority itself that prepares the way for superiority. We may be inferior because we are lazy or because we make poor or morally questionable decisions. Jesus accepted an inferior position in that He became a servant. He was "crowned with glory and honor" because He suffered death for us. He is the ideal Servant-Leader.

Hebrews 4:15 adds another dimension. Jesus is superior because He can "sympathize with our weaknesses," having "been tempted in every way, just as we are—yet without sin" (NIV). He is not the only sinless being. There are multitudes of angels who did not sin. And God the Father and the Holy Spirit are love, are absolutely righteous, and are completely opposed to sin. However, no one but Jesus lived on this earth without sinning. He is the only sinless human being.

3. Hebrews 7; 9; and 12

In chapter 7 Jesus is portrayed as the high priest according to the order of Melchizedek. This chapter also states that He is superior because He is "holy, innocent, undefiled, separated from sinners, higher than the heavens" (7:26, NAB). Jesus is superior because He led a holy life, lived victoriously, and served others with all His heart.

The "better sacrifices" of Hebrews 9:23 refers to Jesus' sacrifice.[8] And according to Hebrews 12:24, Jesus is superior to Abel. Both died as martyrs, but it is only through Christ's death that humankind can be saved. The blood of Abel cries for vengeance (Gen. 4:10). The blood of Jesus opens the way into the heavenly sanctuary.

Jesus instituted a new covenant between God and humanity and is the Mediator of this covenant. He is the only One who by virtue of His personal experience can understand both sides. He is God and can represent the Almighty. He is human and can represent us. Jesus' unparalleled service on earth led to His superiority in status, which in turn led to superiority in His present ministry (8:6).

III. The Results of Jesus' Superior Ministry

We will focus on only those outcomes and blessings that are described with a noun and an adjective in the comparative form. Seven texts demand our attention.

Hebrews 7:19 speaks of a better hope. And Hebrews 7:22 and 8:6 mention a better covenant. The latter verse contains three comparatives, which point to the much more excellent ministry of Jesus, the better covenant, and better promises. Hebrews 9:13, 14 emphasizes a better cleansing. Chapter 10:34 adds "a better possession," and chapter 11:16 mentions "a better country, that is, a heavenly one." Finally, Hebrews 11:35 introduces the idea of "a better resurrection" (NASB). An eighth text uses the adjective in its comparative form as a noun. God has planned something better for us (Heb. 11:40). The term *covenant* is important. It is the only item to be mentioned twice. The other terms are all related to the covenant. A covenant contains obligations and promises—blessings for those who meet the obligations and curses for those who neglect them. The promises of the Abrahamic covenant included the divine presence, a blessing for all families of the earth, becoming a great nation, receiving a great name, and a homeland.[9] While these promises resemble those of the new covenant, the latter surpass them.

The better hope "concerns what the law and its priesthood had failed to realize and could only point forward to in a symbolic way, namely, direct and lasting access to God. Through this 'better hope' the new people of God have secured the assurance of a quality of access to and a relationship with God that were not possible under the Levitical institution."[10] Paul emphasizes the better cleansing and perfect forgiveness when he discusses the new covenant more extensively (see Heb. 8:6-13; esp. verse 12).

In Hebrews 10:34, Paul praises the church members for having endured persecution and the loss of their property, assuring them that they have "a better and lasting possession." Jesus told His disciples that treasures that are stored in heaven cannot be destroyed or stolen (Matt. 6:19-21). "The goal of believers, elsewhere expressed as rest (4:9, 11) . . . or the heavenly city (11:16; 12:27), is here described in terms of property."[11] Under the new covenant the promise of the land given to Abraham in Genesis 12 will be fulfilled on a much larger scale. Paul knows that Abraham "sojourned in the promised land as in a foreign country" (11:9, NAB) and expected a heavenly homeland, the better land (11:16). Indeed, "God had foreseen something better" (11:40), the fullness of salvation that was and will be realized through Jesus our Lord. The followers of Jesus have already come to the heavenly Jerusalem (12:22) and yet are longing for the lasting city (13:14), the better homeland. According to John, Jesus is preparing this place for us and will come and take us to Himself (John 14:1-3).

Finally, there is a better resurrection (Heb 11:35). This better resurrection is the final resurrection, different from all previous resurrections mentioned in the Bible, which returned people to temporary, mortal life. The better resurrection will raise people to everlasting life. Death will finally be defeated.

Jesus' superior ministry affects us here and now and has far-reaching implications for our future. We already benefit from the blessings—a better hope, better promises, a better covenant, a better and lasting possession, a better country, and a better resurrection—and will experience them fully when the city of the living God is physically present. Jesus gives meaning to our life today, and He provides us a bright future.

IV. Our Reaction to Christ's Superiority

There are only two possible responses to Jesus' superiority in status and ministry. Either we accept Him wholeheartedly or we reject Him. Indifference is no better than total rejection.

Hebrews contrasts the positive reaction with the negative. Chapter 10:29 tells of people who trample Jesus underfoot and despise His blood. They know who the Lord is and what He has done in their lives. They have tasted His goodness and have rejoiced in salvation, but then deliberately turn against God. "They are crucifying the Son of God all over again" (6:6, NIV). This apostasy is the special danger faced by those to whom the letter to the Hebrews was addressed—and by Christians today. "A man who has violated the law of Moses dies without mercy at the testimony of two or three witnesses. How much worse punishment do you think will be deserved by the man who has spurned the Son of God, and profaned the blood of the covenant by which he was sanctified, and outraged the Spirit of grace?" (10:28, 29)

Hebrews 12:25 contains a warning, moving from the lesser to the greater. Whoever intentionally ignores the final revelation of God through His Son and shows contempt for the blessings associated with it cannot escape judgment.

But we need not be among those who turn from God. There is another option. Hebrews mentions Abel twice. Chapter 12:24 compares Jesus' blood to that of Abel. He honored God by bringing a better sacrifice than Cain did (11:4). Abel had a faith relationship with God and so is called righteous. He is the first hero of faith listed in Hebrews 11 and was the very first martyr. Abel relied on the Lord's provisions for his salvation and obeyed Him because he believed in Him.

Similarly, Moses made a decision for Jesus. He rather (literally "much more") chose to suffer with God's people than to enjoy sin (11:25). Moses had his priorities straight. He considered the reproach of Christ greater riches than the treasures of Egypt. He willingly accepted the Lord's superiority.

The examples of Abel and Moses challenge us to choose that which really counts, that which is lasting. Their examples tell us: Choose Christ and do not give up on Him! He is the genuine Lord. His ministry on our behalf is unsurpassed.

Conclusion

Hebrews has a special interest in the topic of superiority. Paul applies this concept to God the Father, His Word, the heavenly sanctuary, and especially Jesus. In Hebrews he presents Jesus' superiority in status—He is, for example, more exalted than are the angels—and His superiority in ministry—His better sacrifice and His ministry in heaven as our high priest. The results are a better covenant, a better hope, a better country, and a better resurrection.

It is not wrong to strive for something that is superior. To the contrary, the Epistle to the Hebrews encourages us to take a hold of that which is better. But the better things are not material possessions, a splendid career, or fame. The better things are the good gifts of our Lord and most of all of Himself. Therefore, we commit ourselves to Him who has brought about "such a great salvation."

---

1. Siegfried Horn, *Seventh-day Adventist Bible Dictionary,* 765, 766.
2. According to Heb. 9:21, the heavenly things of verse 23 are the tabernacle and its vessels.

3. In Heb. 1:5 we read "For to which of the angels did [God] ever say . . ." (NASB) and in 1:13 we find an almost identical phrase. On the other hand, the beginning of 2:5 is very similar to the beginning of 2:16: "For not angels . . ."

4. See Albert Vanhoye, *Structure and Message,* 49–59.

5. Hebrews 3 and 4 contain a strong concentration on the Greek word family *pist-*. The adjective is found in 3:2, 5 in addition to 2:17 and means "faithful" or "believing." The noun *apistia* describes unbelief and unfaithfulness (3:12, 19), whereas the noun *pistis* (4:2) denotes faithfulness, faith, and belief. Finally, the verb occurs in 4:3 and means "to believe," "to have faith," and "to trust."

6. See the many common words in 2:17, 18 and 4:15, 16, especially the terms *high priest, merciful/mercy,* and to *help/help.*

7. Heb. 5:9 starts "and having been made perfect/completed" (NASB) or "having reached his goal/finished his work" (see Luke 13:32). It clearly refers back to verse 7, which mentions Jesus' death. Jesus has finished what He set out to do.

8. The context clearly discusses Christ's sacrifice. In Heb. 9:26 the very same word is used.

9. Gerhard F. Hasel, *Covenant in Blood* (Nampa, Idaho: Pacific Press, 1982), 45–49; see Gen 12:1-3.

10. Lane, *Hebrews 1–8*, 186.

11. Ellingworth, 549.

CHAPTER 5

Jesus, Our High Priest

"Andy Woodland writes: Working as Bible translators in Asia, we had come to two verses spoken by Jesus to His disciples: 'I will pray the Father, and he will give you another Counselor . . .' (John 14:16, RSV) and 'In that day you will ask in my name; and I do not say to you that I shall pray the Father for you' (John 16:26, RSV). Our immediate thought was to use the common vernacular for 'pray' or 'beg,' but our cotranslator had a better idea. 'Use the phrase *do paraat,*' he suggested. 'It's a recommendation an influential person brings in behalf of some-one else.' Not until a trip to the hospital in our adopted country did I fully understand its meaning.

"My wife, Ellie, and I had been asked to help a friend's daughter experiencing post-natal complications. Ellie found the girl, her mother, and mother-in-law waiting in the ward. I stayed outside with the father. Immediately, he turned to me and said, 'You must tell Ellie to speak to the doctor and *do paraat* on my daughter's behalf. We are just poor people from a minority group. They won't respect us or treat us well. But if you *do paraat,* they will give us proper treatment.' Ellie agreed, not knowing if it would make a difference. Thankfully, the doctors did listen and the girl recovered quickly. For us, it was a humbling illustra-tion of how Jesus comes before the Father on our behalf."[1]

So far we have encountered Jesus as king, as the Son of God, and as our brother. Now we are ready to study more closely His priestly mission. Hebrews 5a and 7 develop Jesus' function as our high priest. Hebrews 5b and 6, on the other hand, contain admonitions and warnings. The latter part of chapter 6 brings the heavenly sanctuary into view and speaks of the "anchor of the soul, firm and secure. It enters the inner sanctuary behind the curtain" (6:19, NIV). The last verse of chapter 6 returns to Jesus, our High Priest (6:20).

I. Jesus' Priesthood, the Unique Perspective of Hebrews

The Epistle to the Hebrews tells us some things about Jesus' priesthood that are not found anywhere else in the New Testament. In the first place, the vocabulary differs. Paul used three terms in Hebrews to describe Christ's priestly ministry—*priest, high priest,* and *priesthood.* These terms are not used of Christ anywhere else in the New Testament.

Paul used the term *priest* and related terms thirty-five times in the book of Hebrews. Although the terms are also used of the Levitical priesthood and the priesthood of Melchizedek, the context is always the priesthood of Jesus. His priesthood is compared to those of Melchizedek and Aaron. Nowhere in Hebrews are believers called priests or a priesthood. Jesus is referred to as a priest five times in Hebrews. Three times out of the five, the same Old Testament quotation is applied to Him (Ps. 110:4; in Heb. 5:6; 7:17, 21). He is not just the priest but also the *great priest* (Heb. 10:21). In addition, Jesus is called *high priest* ten times.[2] He is also the *great high priest* (4:14). Finally, His *priesthood* is mentioned once (7:24).

Second, Psalm 110 is quoted quite frequently elsewhere in the New Testament, but it is always the first verse of that chapter to which the authors refer.[3] Hebrews is the only New Testament book that contains references to verse four as well as verse one.[4] Hebrews and Psalm 110 both present Jesus the Messiah as the priest-king.

Third, as Hebrews 8:1, 2 makes clear, the author of this letter is interested in the ministry of Jesus as our high priest following His life on earth. Paul wanted his readers to know that the Cross was not the end of Christ's ministry on our behalf; we need not turn from the crucified Jesus to find help. Lindars suggests that the term *high priest* forms a connection to the Day of Atonement,[5] because it was the high priest who was involved in the service of that day. However, Hebrews does not limit Jesus' ministry to this special phase only. It is interested in the overall picture of Jesus as the priest who serves us.

II. Jesus and the Aaronic Priesthood

Although references to the priesthood of Christ can be found throughout the letter to the Hebrews with the exception of chapters 1 and 11, the topic is especially developed in chapters 5 and 7. Chapter 5 compares Christ's high-priestly ministry with that of the Levitical high priest, while in chapter 7 the focus is His priesthood according to the order of Melchizedek. (Hebrews 5:6, 10 does introduce the order of Melchizedek, but the theme is not developed in that chapter.)

Hebrews 4:14-16 portrays Jesus as the merciful high priest through whom we have access to the throne of grace, which we can approach confidently. In light of this, Paul encourages us to "hold fast to our confession" (vs. 14, NASB). These verses announce the perspective to be developed in chapter 5:1-10. Lane has suggested the following helpful outline:[6]

Hebrews 5:1-10

- A The old office of high priest (5:1)
  - B The solidarity of the high priest with the people (5:2-3)
    - C The humility of the high priest (5:4)
    - C' The humility of Christ (5:5-6)
  - B' The solidarity of Christ with the people (5:7-8)
- A' The new office of high priest (5:9-10)

Aaron's priesthood and the priesthood of Christ have both similarities and differences. Both Jesus and Aaron are human. Both were chosen by God. As mediators, they represent humankind before God. They offer sacrifices. In Aaron's case the sacrifices were mainly animals that were slaughtered and burned or eaten. Hebrews 5 notes Jesus' sacrifices: "Jesus offered up prayers and supplications, with loud cries and tears" (verse 7). "He learned obedience through what he suffered" (verse 8). The phrase in 5:9 "being made perfect" seems to refer to His death on the cross, which was His supreme sacrifice and which is more clearly referred to in other places in Hebrews. Both Aaron's service and Jesus' ministry were "for the sins" of humanity; thus, they performed an atoning service. Both dealt gently, mercifully, and patiently with sinners. Both were humble and did not usurp their priesthood.

Now for the differences: Jesus is the divine Son of God. This crucial point is emphasized in Hebrews 5:5, 6. Jesus served as a priest according to the order of Melchizedek. And Jesus' sacrifice is unique, unrepeated, and sufficient for all humankind. And because it is forever valid and effective, it cannot be replaced by any other. Whereas Aaron offered animals, Jesus offered Himself. In addition to being Priest, Jesus is King, Creator, Sustainer, the One who represents God, and Redeemer. He surpasses Aaron by far. And while Aaron had to sacrifice not only for the people but also for himself (5:2, 3), Jesus' ministry is not weakened by sin.

Both the Levitical priests and Jesus are said to have dealt sympathetically with sinners. However, the Bible makes clear that Levitical priests could be rude, faithless, and wicked (see, e.g., Lev. 10:1, 2; 1 Sam. 1:13, 14; 2:12, 22; Jer. 2:8; 5:31; 6:13; 23:11; 26:8). Priests were responsible for Jesus' execution and the persecution of His followers. Hebrews stresses, on the other hand, the mercy and faithfulness of Jesus, the true High Priest. He sympathizes with us and helps us. However, this sympathy is not sentimentalism that overlooks all mistakes and sins and does not take God's will seriously. It is mercy that provides forgiveness for those who are determined to follow Jesus. A further distinction is that Aaron served on earth, while Jesus serves in heaven. Jesus serves in the real temple and not just its counterpart.

Hebrews 5 ends with three important statements that will be developed later: (1) Jesus has been made perfect, (2) He became the Source of eternal salvation, and (3) He is High Priest according to the order of Melchizedek (5:9, 10). This leads us to Hebrews 7.

III. Jesus and the Priesthood of Melchizedek

Jesus is uniquely qualified to serve as our high priest: He is God's Son; only He shares both divinity and humanity; He has lived among us and died in our place on the cross. So, He is by nature the only perfect Mediator of the universe. But there's a problem. God restricted Israel's priesthood to the male descendants of Aaron, who came from the tribe of Levi, while Jesus' ancestry lay in the tribe of Judah.

Consequently, Paul has to prove from Scripture that Jesus has the right to be not only King but also Priest. Therefore, he points out that Jesus fulfills Psalm 110:4. He is a priest of a different order.

Paul discusses the priesthood of Melchizedek primarily in Hebrews 7. Aside from Hebrews, only two passages in Scripture mention Melchizedek: Genesis 14:18-20 and Psalm 110:4. The first describes Melchizedek's encounter with Abraham. The second is a Messianic prophecy and focuses more on the Messiah than on Melchizedek. The first part of Hebrews 7 explains the Genesis 14 story. The second part expounds on Psalm 110:4, showing its fulfillment in Jesus.

Hebrews 7

1. Melchizedek meets Abraham: Melchizedek's superiority (7:1-10)
   (a) Melchizedek as priest-king (7:1-3)
   (b) Melchizedek is superior because he receives Abraham's tithe (7:4-10)

2. Jesus serves as priest according to Melchizedek's order: His superiority (7:11-28)
   (a) The question of perfection (7:11-19)
   (b) Priesthood and oath (7:20-28)

1. Melchizedek and Abraham (Hebrews 7:1-10)

The first three verses of Hebrews 7 tell a little about the priest-king Melchizedek. He blessed Abraham and received his tithe. After verse 2 explains his name, verse 3 adds some details that are not found in Genesis 14: "Without father, mother, or ancestry, without beginning of days or end of life, like the Son of God he remains a priest forever" (NAB).

This verse has caused some Christians to consider Melchizedek to be a heavenly being—perhaps even Jesus Himself. But we must be careful. Scripture portrays Melchizedek as a historical figure who lived at the time of Abraham. The Greek word translated "without ancestry" may explain the words "without father, mother" as meaning simply that his genealogy is unknown. The text itself indicates that he is not Jesus. It says that he is "made to resemble the Son of God." In other words, he is not the Son of God; he is merely, in some respects, similar to Him.

What about the words "without beginning of days or end of life" and "he remains a priest forever"? "He [Melchizedek] is not eternal in his own right. But in the narrative Melchizedek is *made to resemble* the Son of God, the only one who truly remains priest forever. Melchizedek is like Christ in the sense that Scripture does not provide any record of his birth, his genealogy, or his death. That absence of this information in the biblical account is used by the apostle to liken Melchizedek to Christ, who is indeed eternal."[7]

Hebrews 7 focuses primarily on Jesus. Paul is interested in Melchizedek only because he wants to show that Jesus is rightfully called priest and that His priesthood surpasses the Levitical priesthood.

Verses 4-10 point out that Abraham paid his tithe to Melchizedek and was blessed by him. Since "a lesser person is blessed by a greater," Melchizedek is greater than Abraham. By implication, then, he is also greater than Abraham's descendants, the Levitical priests. In Abraham they too paid tithe to Melchizedek (vss. 4-10). In Abraham they were blessed. So, Melchizedek's priesthood surpasses the Levitical priesthood.

2. Christ and Melchizedek (Hebrews 7:11-28)

The second part of Hebrews 7 draws conclusions from the arguments presented in the first part. The author begins by showing that the Levitical system did not bring about perfection. Thus the law that instituted the Aaronic priests was superseded by the promise of Psalm 110:4. Jesus is the genuine High Priest; He is the One who fulfills the Old Testament prophecy.

When Paul had explained the phrase "the order of Melchizedek," he could interpret the other elements of Psalm 110:4. God has undergirded the new priesthood by an oath. This priesthood is limited to one person; multiple priests are unnecessary because Jesus' priesthood is permanent.

Verses 25-28 describe the point of Jesus' priesthood. While the Levitical priesthood could not bring about perfection, this perfection has come through Jesus. The Son "has been made perfect forever" (7:28). Because Jesus is the Son, He is superior to Moses (chapter 3) and Aaron (chapter 5) and is a priest according to the order of Melchizedek, whom He also surpasses.

IV. Jesus' Characteristics as High Priest

The characteristics of Jesus as priest and high priest are discussed not only in Hebrews 7 but also in a number of other places.

1. Jesus is eternal (7:24, 25). He is not limited by death as are the Levitical priests. His throne stands forever (1:8). He is a priest forever (5:6; 6:20; 7:17, 21). He "has been made perfect forever" (7:28). "Jesus Christ is the same yesterday and today and forever" (13:8). What He did for us as sacrifice and priest will affect us forever. We can rely on Him. Therefore, to Him "be glory for ever and ever" (13:21).

2. Jesus cares for others; He is not self-centered (7:25). Chapter 2:17 says He is merciful and faithful, and the following chapters develop these two characteristics in reverse order: they show that Jesus is as faithful as Moses was—though He surpasses Moses—and they expand on His mercifulness (4:14–5:10).

3. Jesus is holy (7:26). Greek has two words that mean "holy": *hagios* and *hosios*. It uses the term *hagios* for the Holy Spirit,[8] for the sanctuary with its apartments,[9] and for Christians,[10] reserving the term *hosios* for Jesus alone. Chapter 7:26 is the only place in which Hebrews calls Jesus holy. Here, it distinguishes Jesus from human beings.[11] Although Jesus was made sin for us, He did not sin at all. So His holiness is qualitatively different from the holiness that is ascribed to us. Therefore, His holiness is best named by a term different from that which names ours.[12]

4. Jesus is called "holy, innocent, undefiled" (7:26, NASB). His innocence points to a moral quality. He was guileless in His relationship with others and untouched by evil. "Taken together these three adjectives describe the sinlessness of the high priest. . . . In contrast to the Levitical high priest, of whom there was demanded only ritual purity (Lev. 21:11) and bodily integrity (Lev. 21:17), the high priest appropriate to the Christian community was qualified by spiritual and moral perfection."[13]

5. Jesus is "higher than the heavens" (7:26, NAB), and yet "he offered himself" as a sacrifice (7:27). Humility accompanies His superiority. Although He was the Son of God, He "did not take upon himself the glory of becoming a high priest" (5:5, NIV). The Father installed Him in that office.

6. Jesus has been made perfect (7:28). In this process, however, Jesus was not passive. He had to endure trials and suffering and be faithful and obedient to God no matter what. He never gave up His relationship to God or withdrew from God—not even momentarily.

7. Jesus is Lord and servant. He is willing to serve, to mediate, to intervene, to listen to us and help us. The servant concept is part of the motif of the priesthood. It is repeated in chapter 8:2.

Although Jesus is holy and eternally perfect, exalted above the heavens, He turns toward us weak, sinful, erring beings to save us. We, then, are challenged not only to accept Jesus as our Savior and Lord but also to take Him as our example and, as disciples, to follow His footsteps.

V. Jesus' Work and Function as High Priest

We now return to Jesus' functions as our high priest.

1. Jesus offered Himself as a sacrifice (7:27). Without a sacrifice no high-priestly ministry is possible. The priesthood depends on the sacrifice. Jesus applies His blood and His righteousness to us.

2. Jesus is able and willing to "expiate the sins of the people" (2:17, NAB). He provides the only possible solution for the sin problem.

3. Jesus has opened the way to the throne of grace (4:15, 16). We now have direct access to God. We can address God in boldness and confidence and yet reverently.

4. Jesus sympathizes with us (4:15). Many of us suffer from an intense loneliness, from desperation, from a sense of meaninglessness, though we may hide our pain. We desire to be loved, to be cared for, and to have hope beyond death. This is what the High Priest offers us.

5. Jesus saves. "He is able to save completely those who come to God through him" (7:25, NIV). He applies His death on the cross to those who believe in Him and will also bring about the final consummation and salvation.

6. "He always lives to intercede for them" (7:25, NIV). Jesus works as our mediator and intercessor. Whereas other priests attempt to reconcile estranged parties, only Jesus' mediation is effective.

7. Jesus' ministry as our high priest is objective. It does not depend on how we feel or think. We can focus on Him instead of on us. Although there are subjective elements in the Christian life, our faith is based on what Jesus has done and is doing for us right now.

Conclusion

Some of us are troubled by the fact that we commit the same sin over and over again. Others, although they've become indifferent to certain sins, know their relationship to God is faulty. And still others fear to approach the throne of grace. However, there is a High Priest to whom we may turn. He is willing to intercede for us. Christianity does not affect only the past and the future. It impacts our lives here and now. We can experience its benefits.

1. Craig Brian Larson, *Choice Contemporary Stories and Illustrations for Preachers, Teachers, and Writers* (Grand Rapids: Baker Book House, 1998), 139.
2. Heb. 2:17; 3:1; 4:14,15; 5:5,10; 6:20; 7:26; 8:1; 9:11.
3. Direct quotations are found in Matt. 22:44; Mark 12:36; Luke 20:42, 43; Acts 2:34, 35; Heb. 1:13. Yet, a number of other texts, such as 1 Cor. 15:25; Heb. 1:3; 8:1; 10:12, allude to Ps. 110:4.
4. Ps. 110:4 is quoted in Heb. 5:6; 7:17, 21 and alluded to in Heb. 5:10; 6:20; 7:3, 11, 15.
5. See Lindars, 61, 62, 72.
6. Lane, *Hebrews 1–8,* 111.
7. Angel M. Rodriguez, "Melchizedek: Human or Divine?" *Adventist Review,* August 10, 2000, p. 11.
8. Heb. 2:4; 3:7; 6:4; 10:15.
9. E.g., Heb. 9:12, 24, 25.
10. Heb. 3:1; 6:10; 13:24.
11. For more information, see Lane, *Hebrews 1–8,* 191.
12. Of the use of this term concerning God, Friedrich Hauck states: "He and he alone is worthy to be praised and perfectly blameless, maintaining righteousness and truth without abridgment or disruption, and bringing salvation by His acts." See "ὅsios" in *Theological Dictionary of the New Testament,* Gerhard Kittel, ed. (Grand Rapids: Wm. B. Eerdmans Publishing Company, 1983), 5:491, 492.
13. Lane, *Hebrews 1–8,* 192.

Sanctuary Language in Hebrews

In December 1989 the *Moody Monthly* reported regarding the Jerusalem temple: "Several small organizations intent on rebuilding the temple received additional publicity, and perhaps credibility, in October when Israel's Religious Affairs Ministry sponsored the first conference of Temple Research. One of the most zealous groups is the Temple Institute, which has reconstructed 38 of the 103 ritual implements required for sacrifices. 'Our task is to advance the cause of the temple and to prepare for its establishment, not just talk about it,' says director Zev Golan. 'No one can say how, and no one wants to do it by force. But sooner or later, in a week or in a century, it will be done.' Two Talmudic schools near the Western (Wailing) Wall are teaching students details of temple service. Other scholars are researching genealogies to identify members of the priestly line."[1]

Centuries after the destruction of the Jerusalem temple by the Romans there is still interest in the earthly sanctuary and its rituals. The book of Hebrews is full of sanctuary language. In some places this language refers to the earthly sanctuary, in other places to the heavenly. Jesus is the fulfillment of the Old Testament sanctuary system. His ministry is portrayed in sanctuary language. Since the sanctuary doctrine includes the crucifixion and high-priestly ministry of Jesus Christ, we want to learn all we can about it.

I. Sanctuary Vocabulary Used in Hebrews

The following table displays the sanctuary vocabulary of Hebrews. Some terms are used in connection with the sanctuary but also in a more general way. I have not listed those places in which a particular word is used in a more general sense, unrelated to the sanctuary. The table may not be complete.

Sanctuary terms	**References**
The Sanctuary Itself	
Sanctuary	8:2; 9:1, 2, 8, 12, 24, 25; 10:19; 13:11
The Most Holy Place	9:3
Tabernacle	8:2, 5; 9:2, 3, 6, 8, 11, 21; 13:10
Throne	1:8; 4:16; 8:1; 12:2
Important Furnishings of the Sanctuary	
Altar	7:13; 13:10
Ark of the covenant	9:4
Golden altar of incense	9:4
Lampstand	9:2
Mercy seat, place of expiation	9:5
Table	9:2
Veil	6:19; 9:3; 10:20
Accessories of the Sanctuary	
Aaron's rod	9:4
Blood	9:7, 12, 13, 14, 18, 19, 20, 21, 22, 25; 10:4, 19, 29; 11:28; 12:24; 13:11, 12, 20
Bread of the Presence	9:2
Burnt offering	10:6, 8
Crimson wool	9:19
Drink	9:10
Food	9:10; 13:9
Gifts	5:1; 8:3, 4; 9:9; 11:4
Manna jar	9:4

Hyssop	9:19
Sacrifice	5:1; 7:27; 8:3; 9:9, 23, 26; 10:1, 5, 8, 11, 12, 26; 11:4; 13:15, 16
Sin offering	10:6, 8; 13:11
Tables of the covenant	9:4
Vessels	9:21
Washings	9:10

Sacrificial Animals

Bull	9:13; 10:4
Calf, young bull	9:12, 19
Goat	9:12, 13, 19; 10:4
Heifer	9:13

Actions Related to the Sanctuary

Cleansing, purifying	9:14, 22, 23; 10:2
Cleansing, purification	1:3
Purification, purity[2]	9:13
Expiating	2:17
Offering	5:1, 3, 7; 8:3, 4; 9:7, 9, 14, 25, 28; 10:1, 2, 8, 11, 12; 11:4, 17
Sanctifying	2:11; 9:13; 10:10, 14, 29; 13:12
Saving	7:25
Salvation	1:14; 2:3, 10; 5:9; 6:9; 9:28; 11:7
Serving, worshiping	8:5; 9:9; 10:2; 13:10
Service, worship	9:1, 6
Serving, worshiping	10:11
Service, worship[3]	8:6; 9:21
Setting free, releasing	13:23
Release, deliverance	9:15; 11:35
Sprinkling	9:13, 19, 21; 10:22

The Problem and the Solution

Covenant, testament	7:22; 8:6, 8, 9, 10; 9:4, 15, 16, 17, 20; 10:16, 29; 12:24; 13:20

Redemption	9:12
Sin	1:3; 2:17; 3:13; 4:15; 5:1, 3; 7:27; 8:12; 9:26, 28; 10:2, 3, 4, 6, 8, 11, 12, 17, 18, 26; 11:25; 12:1, 4; 13:11

(see also under Actions)

Persons Related to the Sanctuary

Cherubim	9:5
High priest	2:17; 3:1; 4:14, 15; 5:1, 5, 10; 6:20; 7:26, 27, 28; 8:1, 3; 9:7, 11, 15; 13:11
Priest	5:6; 7:1, 3, 11, 14, 15, 17, 20, 21, 23; 8:4; 9:6; 10:11, 21
Priesthood	7:5
Priesthood[4]	7:11, 12, 24
Mediator	8:6; 9:15; 12:24
Servant, minister	8:2

This list contains about 240 references and reveals how important the topic of the sanctuary is in Hebrews. At the same time it shows that some terms are used much more frequently than others.

Terms	**Frequency**	**Remarks**
Tabernacle	9 times	6 times in Heb. 9
Sanctuary and Most Holy Place	11 times	8 times in Heb. 9
Priest	14 times	9 times in Heb. 7
Sacrifice	15 times	6 times in Heb. 10, not counting different types of offerings
High priest	17 times	Almost evenly distributed in chapters 2–9, 13
Covenant/testament	17 times	5 times in Heb. 8, and 7 times in Heb. 9

To offer	19 times	Most frequently in Heb. 9 and 10
Blood	21 times	Most frequently in Heb. 9, namely 11 times
Sin	25 times	Most frequently in Heb. 10, namely 8 times

The word *priest* and related words appear thirty-five times in Hebrews. Obviously, then, priesthood comprises a dominant theme in this epistle. *Sanctuary* and *tabernacle,* combined, appear twenty times. And *sin* and *blood* are employed together even more often.

Priesthood	-	35 times
Sin	-	25 times
Blood	-	21 times
Sanctuary	-	20 times

Word frequency may—or may not—help in determining the main theme of a letter. Therefore, it would not be accurate to claim that priesthood and/or sanctuary comprise the main topic of Hebrews. The many warnings[5] and the announcements of judgment[6] found in the letter suggest the author may have been primarily concerned with warning us that if we leave Jesus, we forfeit our salvation. However, the concept of priesthood aids in the development of this main topic. This explains why the author mentions only certain aspects of the priesthood—those that are crucial for his main theme. In his argumentation he moves from the inferior to the greater and develops the superiority of Christ and His ministry.

The distribution of sanctuary vocabulary in the different chapters of Hebrews is revealing too. Hebrews 7 uses words from this vocabulary twenty-one times. Hebrews 8 employs them twenty-four times. Hebrews 9 surpasses all other chapters with eighty-five usages, and Hebrews 10 uses the vocabulary forty-three times. The next table shows the distribution of the most important sanctuary words throughout Hebrews 7–10.

Sanctuary Language in Hebrews

Chapter	Important Terms	Frequency
Heb. 7	Priest and high priest	12 times
Heb. 8	Covenant	5 times
Heb. 9	Tabernacle and sanctuary	14 times
	Blood	11 times
	Covenant/testament	7 times
	To offer	5 times
Heb. 10	Sin	8 times
	Sacrifice	6 times
	To offer	5 times

This table seems to indicate that Hebrews 7 focuses on the priesthood, Hebrews 8 on the covenant, Hebrews 9 on the sanctuary and its service, and Hebrews 10 on the sacrifice for sin. The central chapters of Hebrews seem to be chapters 9 and 10.

II. The Sanctuary

Hebrews uses two different words for the sanctuary, the terms *hagion/hagia* and *skēnē*. The first word is an adjective and means "holy." In Hebrews it is used as a noun and is translated "sanctuary," "Holy Place," and "Most Holy Place." It usually denotes the entire sanctuary rather than the Most Holy Place. The second word means "tent" or "tabernacle" and refers to the Old Testament tabernacle that served Israel before the temple was built. In Hebrews 10:21 the additional term *house* may also refer to the sanctuary as it does in other New Testament texts.[7] However, nowhere else in Hebrews does it refer to the sanctuary.

In using *hagion/hagia,* Hebrews avoids using the standard New Testament vocabulary of terms designating the sanctuary, though the terms Hebrews uses are also found in the Greek Old Testament. The term *skēnē* is rarely used to denote God's tabernacle in the New Testament, though in Revelation it indicates the heavenly tabernacle (Rev. 15:5), and the verb *to tabernacle* points to the fact that God will dwell among His people (Rev. 7:15; 21:3).

Why does the author of Hebrews use this specific vocabulary? We don't know for sure, but here are some possible reasons: (1) Using the term *hagion/hagia* may stress the holiness of the sanctuary. (2) This specific term can be used of the entire sanctuary as well as of the different apartments. In the New Testament, only the Epistle to the Hebrews and the book of Revelation speak of the apartments of the sanctuary.[8] (3) The author is reflecting the Old Testament, which quite often uses *to hagion* to indicate the sanctuary.[9] (4) Daniel employs the same vocabulary (Dan. 8:11, 13, 14; 9:24; 11:31). The desolation of the sanctuary, its anointing, and its cleansing/restoration are mentioned. In addition, in Hebrews 9:23, Paul used the same Greek word for "cleansing" as Daniel used in Daniel 8:14. Daniel was writing about the cleansing of the heavenly sanctuary, and Paul about the cleansing of the heavenly things. Obviously, he was referring to the sanctuary in Hebrews 9:23, because the next verse mentions the sanctuary not made by hands. A connection to Daniel and its sanctuary concept, including the investigative judgment, is possible.[10]

The term *skēnē* is used constantly in Exodus 25–40 when the erection of the Old Testament tabernacle is discussed. It is also the standard term in Leviticus and Numbers and is found in the New Testament. *Skēnē* is more useful than other sanctuary terms, because it stands for the original sanctuary, the tabernacle, which corresponds with the heavenly original and is not embellished by additional furnishings as was the later temple. The term *skēnē* may relate a special closeness with God that is more clearly depicted in Revelation.

Hebrews mentions the throne four times (1:8; 4:16; 8:1; 12:2). The context of Hebrews 4:16; 8:2 indicates that the throne is found in the sanctuary (cp. Ps.11:4; Isa. 6:1; Rev. 7:15; 16:17). The sanctuary, God's dwelling place, is the center of His government. Salvation, assistance, and judgment proceed from His sanctuary. In fact, the Old Testament term for temple *(hēkāl)* is also translated "palace."

III. Important Furnishings and Accessories

Hebrews mentions all the basic temple furnishings: the lampstand, the table, the altars, and the ark of the covenant. The sanctuary that

Paul had in mind was the original one that God revealed and which was built under Moses' supervision (Exod. 25–31; 35–40). Solomon's temple was more elaborate and contained more of the various pieces of furniture—for instance, ten golden lampstands and ten tables. The huge Herodian temple of the time of Jesus was lacking the ark of the covenant.

Although Hebrews points to all the basic furnishings of the earthly sanctuary and even goes into some details such as relating to us the content of the ark of the covenant, it does not describe the furnishings of the heavenly temple. The author of Hebrews is convinced that heaven contains a real sanctuary in which Jesus is ministering on our behalf. This sanctuary certainly surpasses our understanding and imagination, and we need to be careful not to restrict it in one way or another beyond what the Bible tells us, because our senses and our minds are limited.

IV. Sacrifices

Hebrews lists four different kinds of sacrificial animals (Heb. 9:12, 13, 19; 10:4). With the exception of the heifer *(damalis),* they come in pairs, "goats *(tragoi)* and calves *(moschoi)*" and "goats *(tragoi)* and bulls *(tauroi).*" The lamb, which is so prominent in Revelation, is not found in Hebrews.

Some scholars claim that Hebrews' mention of the goats and bulls/calves indicates Paul was focusing on the Day of Atonement, and that the Day of Atonement has been fulfilled on the cross. The Septuagint was the Greek translation of the Old Testament that Paul used in Hebrews. Its translation of Leviticus 16 mentions three types of animals and uses the following terms: bull *(moschos),*[11] ram *(krios),*[12] and male goat *(chimaros).*[13] *Ram* occurs only twice; *bull* is found eight times; and *goat* occurs fourteen times. The concept of the blood of bulls and goats is found in both Leviticus 16 and Hebrews 9. Thus, Hebrews 9, 10 may well hint at the Day of Atonement.

Yet these chapters in Hebrews do not use the precise language with regard to the sacrifices of the Day of Atonement. The ram is missing. And whereas Leviticus 16 uses *chimaros* of the he-goat, Hebrews 9 uses *tragos. Chimaros* is found quite often in the Old Testament; it means the sin offering.[14] Interestingly enough, in Numbers 7 the *chimaros* (he-goat) and the *tragos* (goat) stand next to each other. The *chimaros* represents a sin offering; the *tragoi,* mentioned thirteen times, represent peace offerings. The situation is the dedication of the sanctuary, which seems to be reflected in Hebrews 9:18, 19.

A phrase almost identical to "the blood of goats and bulls" *(to haima tragōn kai taurōn)* as found in Hebrews 9:13 occurs in only one place in the Old Testament—namely, in Isaiah 1:11 (NAB): "the blood of goats and bulls" *(haima tragōn kai taurōn).* This is the closest Old Testament parallel. In Isaiah 1 God says He isn't interested in the blood of goats and bulls because the people's heart is not with Him. This passage is referring to Israel's entire sacrificial system,[15] which may also be the point in Hebrews 9. According to Isaiah 1, blood sacrifices are meaningless as long as those who offer them are not involved personally by turning toward God, repenting of sin, and choosing a "lifestyle of justice and righteousness."[16] In Hebrews 9 and 10, Paul is saying that blood sacrifices of animals are not sufficient. Eternal salvation has been obtained only through the blood of Jesus, through which our consciences are purified "from dead works to serve the living God" (Heb. 9:12, 14).

The language of Hebrews 9:12, 13 indicates that while the Day of Atonement is included, it was not the major focus. This passage has a wider scope. Jesus' sacrifice fulfilled those required for the Day of Atonement. However, from Paul's perspective, Christ's high-priestly ministry as associated with the Day of Atonement was still future.

V. The Problem and Its Solution

Two additional terms are used in Hebrews that refer to the sanctuary: *sin* and *covenant.* Sin is our basic problem. The Fall in Eden changed people's relationship with God and with one another. And because sin brought along disease, suffering, and death, the entire ecosystem has deteriorated. In Romans, Paul points out that sin makes people do evil although they wish to do good. It perverts God's good law, which now must condemn us instead of pointing out the path to a happy life. Sin makes necessary the plan of salvation, including Jesus' death as the ultimate sacrifice and His high-priestly ministry. Sin is at the heart of the sanctuary service.

In Scripture the emphasis is not so much on this problem but on the solution: forgiveness of sin, liberation from sin, and the power to overcome. Hebrews particularly uses the concepts of purification and salvation. Jesus is the only valid Sacrifice and the superior High Priest. The covenant describes what God is doing for our salvation and how we should respond.

VI. Persons Related to the Sanctuary

The people whom the apostle mentions as related to the sanctuary are cherubim, priests, high priests, the minister in the sanctuary, and the mediator. The titles *priest* and *high priest* refer to descendants of Aaron as well as to Jesus. However, He is the ultimate Priest and High Priest. His ministry is the only one that can solve the sin problem. Paul used the term *minister (leitourgos)* of the angels in Hebrews 1:7 (NASB) and of Jesus, the Minister in the heavenly sanctuary. Jesus' ministry (*leitourgia;* 8:6) is the real "liturgy." The word *mediator* is found three times in Hebrews (8:6; 9:15; 12:24) and is applied only to Jesus. There is indeed only one Mediator between God and humankind, Jesus Christ.

The cherubim mentioned in Hebrews 9:5 are the two golden figures placed on the mercy seat in the earthly sanctuary. Cherubim are also found in Ezekiel 1 and 10 and in Revelation 4. They are not just mythological figures; they are real beings (Genesis 3:24) and "appear everywhere in the service of God, and usually in His immediate presence. In poetic, symbolic language they are represented as carrying God, or as guarding or overshadowing His throne."[17] Hebrews strongly opposes angel worship.[18] Perhaps this explains why it does not mention the heavenly counterpart of the cherubim in the Most Holy Place of the earthly sanctuary.

Conclusion

Hebrews is very rich in sanctuary language and concepts. It tells us that God wants to be close to us and dwell among us. Through Jesus we now have access to the Majesty of heaven. This is not to suggest that

God the Father is vindictive, revengeful, and unloving. Jesus confirms that "the Father himself loves" us (John 16:27). However, salvation requires justice as well as love on God's part. Therefore, a Sacrifice and a Mediator are needed. And in Jesus, God has filled this need.

The sanctuary concept makes a real difference in our lives. We know that something is being done for us right now on an objective basis. We also experience subjectively the closeness of God and the love of Jesus in our everyday lives.

---

1. *Moody Monthly,* December 1989, p. 74.
2. A different noun of the same word family is used here.
3. Another Greek word family is used in these verses.
4. Another Greek term is used in these verses.
5. Heb. 2:1; 3:7-19; 5:11–6:6; 10:26, 27; 12:1-24.
6. Heb. 2:2-4; 4:1-13; 6:7, 8; 10:25-39; 12:25-29.
7. For instance, Matt. 23:38.
8. Yet Revelation addresses the apartments only indirectly. Within the NT the clearest reference to apartments in the sanctuary is found in Hebrews, and its author uses the appropriate language.
9. See, for example, Exod. 28:29, 30, 35; Lev. 10:18.
10. The Greek NT lists Dan. 9:24 next to Heb. 9:12. Barbara and Kurt Aland et al., eds. *Novum Testamentum Graece,* 27th edition (Stuttgart: Deutsche Bibelgesellschaft, 1995), 575.
11. Lev. 16:3, 6, 11, 14, 15, 18, 27.
12. Lev. 16:3, 5.
13. Lev. 16:5, 7-10, 15, 18, 20, 21, 22, 26, 27.
14. One can find such a he-goat in the context of the Day of Atonement (fourteen times in Leviticus 16; Num. 29:11), the Festival of the Weeks (Lev. 23:19), the dedication of the sanctuary (thirteen times in Numbers 7, e.g. 7:16), monthly offerings (Num. 28:15), Passover (Num. 28:30), the Festival of the Trumpets (Num. 29:5), the Festival of Booths (eight times in Numbers 29, starting with vs. 16), etc.
15. The Hebrew text refers to the ram, the fatling, the bull, the lamb, and the goat, whereas the Septuagint mentions the ram, the lamb, the bull, and the goat. As noted by John D. W. Watts, *Isaiah 1–33, Word Biblical Commentary* (Waco: Word Books, 1985), 21: "This is a comprehensive list of the types of blood sacrifice."
16. Watts, 20.
17. Siegfried Horn, *Seventh-day Adventist Bible Dictionary,* 79, 202.
18. See Heb. 1:5-14.

CHAPTER 7

Jesus and the Covenant

Elizabeth Achtemeier has written that the marriage vow means: "I will be with you, no matter what happens to us and between us. If you should become blind tomorrow, I will be there. If you achieve no success and attain no status in our society, I will be there. When we argue and are angry, as we inevitably will, I will work to bring us together. When we seem totally at odds and neither of us is having needs fulfilled, I will persist in trying to understand and in trying to restore our relationship. When our marriage seems utterly sterile and going nowhere at all, I will believe that it can work and I will want it to work and I will do my part to make it work. And when all is wonderful and we are happy, I will rejoice over our life together, and continue to strive to keep our relationship growing and strong."[1]

When husband and wife make such a commitment, they have a marriage *covenant.* In the Old Testament, marriage is regarded as a covenant (Mal. 2:14). Furthermore, the covenant that God made with His people is compared to a marriage relationship: God is the husband; the people are His wife (Ezek. 16:8).

Unfortunately, people today have such a faulty idea of covenants that they oftentimes believe they're something they can just walk out of. But this is not what a covenant should be. A covenant is a lasting agreement. It's true that in Old Testament times God's people broke their covenant with God, but He would not give up the covenant. He remained committed.

The covenant between God and His people is one of the important topics in Hebrews. The old covenant was not an end in itself. A new covenant had been predicted. Paul informs us that this new covenant has been inaugurated and is being administered by Jesus Christ.

I. Covenants in the Old Testament and in Hebrews

1. Different Covenants

The Old Testament mentions a number of covenants. In Genesis 6:18 the word *covenant* appears for the first time. Of this, Gerhard Hasel wrote: "God's judgment would come in the form of a world-wide flood. Yet God had still committed Himself to the world He had created. He had not forsaken those who had not forsaken Him. So God . . . made a covenant as an expression of His relationship with Noah. . . . The divine, redemptive purpose of the covenant relationship that had been in operation since the fall (Genesis 3:15) is here renewed."[2]

In Genesis 9:11-13 we find the Noahic covenant after the Flood. A little later we encounter the Abrahamic covenant. Obviously, different stages were involved. In Genesis 12:1-3 we see several covenant blessings. Genesis 15:18 tells us the covenant was ratified. Chapter 17 contains a further discussion on the covenant. Several blessings are mentioned: Abram and Sarai receive new names, and circumcision is introduced as the sign of the covenant.

Exodus 19:5 and 24:7, 8 throw light on the Sinaitic covenant. This covenant was established after Israel had been saved from slavery in Egypt. Salvation precedes covenant-making. Both are God's gracious acts, in which He takes the initiative. God does not gain much, if anything, by making a covenant with us. He showers His blessings upon us, and we—in response—are obedient to His commandments.

Psalm 89:3, 4 reminds us of the Davidic covenant, also found in 2 Samuel 7. The most important aspect in this covenant is the promise of the coming of the Davidic King and Seed—a blessing that was ultimately fulfilled in Jesus Christ. This promise harmonizes with the other seed promises starting with Genesis 3:15 and found again with Abraham (Gen. 12:7), Isaac (Gen. 26:24), and Jacob (Gen. 35:12).

Finally, God promises a new covenant (Jer. 31:31-34). This promise was fulfilled only during New Testament times. It is the starting point for Paul's deliberations on the covenant as found in Hebrews 8, 9, and 10a.

2. Covenant Forms

Covenants played an important role in the ancient Near East. They described the relationship either between a superior power and a subordinate people or between equals. The divine-human covenants mentioned above are clearly covenants between a superior power and inferiors. (A covenant between equals is mentioned in Genesis 31:43, 44.)

According to Hasel, Hittite covenants between superiors and inferiors contained the following elements: "1. Preamble introducing the sovereign. 2. The historical prologue describing previous relations between the contracting parties. 3. The stipulations which outline the nature of the community formed by the covenant treaty. 4. The document clause providing for the preservation and regular rereading of the treaty. 5. The lists of gods who witnessed the treaty. 6. The curse and blessings, or blessing formula—curses depending upon infidelity and blessing upon fidelity to the treaty."[3] Biblical covenants resemble this covenant form; we find, for instance, blessings and curses (Exod. 23:20-33; Leviticus 26; Deuteronomy 28). Yet we must let the Bible define God's covenant with His people.

A sacrifice was mentioned in the context of the Abrahamic covenant (Genesis 15). After God had saved Israel from Egypt, He offered them His covenant, and they responded with the promise: " 'All that the LORD has spoken we will do!' " (Exod. 19:8; 24:7). God explained the promises and gave His law, which they were obliged to keep. Sacrifices were offered, and the covenant was ratified by blood (Exod. 24:8). The covenant laws included the establishment of the sanctuary, the installation of the priesthood, and the formal institution of the sacrificial system (Exodus 25–31). In Exodus 34:27 God refers back to the covenant with Moses and Israel. Thus, covenant, sacrifices, priesthood, and sanctuary belong together.

3. Covenant Promises

In Abraham's case, the covenant promises included the promise of God's constant presence, the Messianic promise as a blessing for all peoples of the earth, and the promise of land and of becoming a great nation. The Mosaic, or Sinaitic, covenant was an enlargement of the earlier covenants. After having saved the Israelites from Egypt, God graciously offered them His covenant and promised to make Israel His treasured possession, a kingdom of priests, and a holy nation.

4. The Covenant in Hebrews

The climax of the letter to the Hebrews is reached with chapters 8–10a. Hebrews 8 stresses the importance of the new covenant, using the term *covenant* five times.[4] Hebrews 9 contrasts the old tabernacle and its service with the heavenly sanctuary and Jesus' sacrifice. His sacrifice was unique, unrepeatable, and sufficient. Introduced in chapter 9, it comprises the central theme of chapter 10a. These different themes—namely covenant, priesthood, and sacrifice—are related, so the theological concept of the new covenant is not limited to chapter 8.

The covenant is first mentioned in Hebrews 7:22, but only in passing. In Hebrews 8 the longest quotation from the Old Testament to appear in the New Testament is added (vss. 8-12), and a brief comment on the covenant is made. Paul quotes the promise of a new covenant, which requires a new priesthood and a better sanctuary. Then he claims that the new priesthood has come in the person of Jesus and says that the better sanctuary is the heavenly sanctuary.

In Hebrews 9:4, the apostle tells us about the ark of the covenant and the tables of the covenant, namely the Ten Commandments. Next, he calls Jesus the Mediator of the new covenant (9:15). He had already used that title in chapter 8:6, but whereas there he linked the concepts of covenant and priesthood, in Hebrews 9 he added another relationship[5]; namely, that of covenant and sacrifice (e.g., 9:12-14, 18). The better covenant requires a better sacrifice, which in turn will allow for a better priesthood. In Hebrews 9:20 we find a quotation from Exodus 24:8. This quotation connects blood, and thus sacrifice, (neither of which is found in Jeremiah 31) to the covenant.

In the practical application section of Hebrews 10 the apostle briefly mentions the blood of the covenant. The Mediator of the new covenant is mentioned in Hebrews 12:24 and the blood of the eternal covenant in chapter 13:20.[6]

II. The Old Covenant and the New Covenant

In Hebrews, Paul calls the Mosaic covenant the first covenant and says it has grown old. He pictures a sharp contrast between this old covenant and the new, better, eternal covenant (Heb. 8:6, 13; 9:15; 13:20). However, in no place does he say that the old covenant was bad or detrimental. It simply was inadequate and needed to be replaced. An outline of Hebrews 8 by Gourges supports these observations:[7]

Hebrews 8

A	Christ, the ministering priest	8:1-5
	1. A new ministry	8:1, 2
	2. which is set in opposition to the old	8:3-5
B	Christ, the mediator of the new covenant	8:6-13
	1. The new ministry is associated with a better covenant	8:6
	2. which is set in opposition to the old	8:7-13

The old covenant and the new covenant have both similarities and differences. The partners in both covenants are the same: God and His people. In both cases, God takes the initiative: He saves. There are promises of blessings and certain duties. The goal of the covenants is to establish God's presence among His people.

The new covenant differs from the old in that it has a new priesthood, a better, once-for-all sacrifice, a better sanctuary, the internalization of the law, and a new worship service or liturgy. The new covenant brings total forgiveness and assurance, real hope, and genuine salvation. This covenant is permanent. It was ratified with the blood of Jesus.

Paul quotes Jeremiah 31 twice in Hebrews: a longer version in 8:8-12 and a shorter one in 10:16, 17. These two quotations parenthetically enclose the high point of the book of Hebrews.

The apostle also stresses the necessity of a change of the law (Heb. 7:12)—namely, the Mosaic law, which was only a shadow of the things to come (10:1, 9). The covenant laws included the establishment of the sanctuary, the installation of the priesthood, and the institution of the sacrificial system (Exodus 25–31). That specific system of law was fulfilled in Jesus and done away with after His death. But another particular law that was part of the old covenant, namely the Decalogue, remains as part of the new covenant. That law is not abolished; rather, it is internalized, written on the heart (Heb. 8:10). When the covenant was made, and later when it was renewed, the Ten Commandments were distinguished from the so-called ordinances (Exod. 21:1; 24:4, 7, 12; 34:27, 28). "The giving of the law is as much an act of mercy as the deliverance from Egyptian slavery. The gift of the law is just as much an act of God's love as the making of the covenant to which the law belongs. . . . God does not speak of a new law, but of a new covenant."[8]

In Hebrews 9:16, 17 a number of translations use the terms *testament* or *will* instead of *covenant*. In Greek the word that means "covenant" also means "testament" or "will." Paul's basic argument is that as a death is required to set a will in force, so the death of Jesus was necessary for the new covenant to be established. The quotation from Exodus 24:8 emphasizes the blood of the covenant.

III. Benefits of the Covenant

Paul wrote that the new covenant has "better promises" (Heb. 8:6). In the New Testament, the term *promise* occurs most frequently in the book of Hebrews. The promises of the new covenant include:

1. access to God (10:19);
2. sanctification (10:10, 14);
3. eternal salvation, especially in the context of Christ's second coming (9:12, 15, 28);
4. a clear conscience (9:9, 14; 10:2);

5. the internalization of the law in our hearts and minds (8:10; 10:16); and

6. forgiveness of sins (8:12; 9:26, 28; 10:17, 18).

Forgiveness of sin is stressed the most and is an important theme running through the entire center part of Hebrews.[9] It is introduced by the quotation taken from Jeremiah 31 and elaborated throughout Hebrews 9 and 10a. The quotation, " 'their sins and their lawless deeds I will remember no more' " (NASB) is repeated in chapter 10:17 and commented on in the next verse.

Some people claim that in arousing guilt, Christianity harms people's emotional and physical health. It is true that the Bible tells us that we are sinners and need a Savior. But it is only Christianity that offers a viable solution for the sin problem. People who have committed their lives to God do not need to worry any longer about their sins. When they have asked God for forgiveness, they can rely on His promises and not on their own feelings. So, only Christians can take sin seriously, oppose it, and yet live happily even if they fall prey to it. They have a Sacrifice and a High Priest—Jesus Christ. Thus, they have a healthier approach to life than does anyone else.

IV. Jesus and the Covenant

In Hebrews, Paul used different adjectives to describe the new covenant. He called it, for instance, the "better" covenant (8:6). In Hebrews 8:8, 13, he used the Greek word *kainos* concerning the covenant, whereas in Hebrews 12:24 he used the word *neos.* Both adjectives are translated "new"; however, there is a slight difference between them. The word *kainos* has the nuance of something that was unheard of, pointing to the marvelous character of the new covenant. The word *neos* carries the sense of being recent. The new covenant is both: brand-new and qualitatively better.

What is most important is not the covenant itself. It is the person who has ratified it and who now ministers in its context. Jesus is the surety of the new covenant. In Hebrews 7:22 (NASB) He is called the guarantee of a better covenant, and three times in Hebrews He appears as the mediator of the better or new covenant (8:6; 9:15; 12:24). The terms *guarantor, guarantee,* or *surety* occur nowhere else in the New Testament. "It is common in the papyri in legal documents in the sense of a pledge or as a reference to bail. . . . Since the covenant in the biblical sense is an agreement initiated by God, the surety (i.e., Jesus) guarantees that that covenant will be honored. . . . The mediator is a go-between whose task is to keep the parties in fellowship with each other."[10]

Those sections of Hebrews that contain admonitions, especially chapters 12 and13, do stress our responsibility, but in general we find a stronger emphasis on what Jesus has been and is doing on our behalf than on what is required of us. Why? The reason may be that Paul wants to help those of his readers who are troubled by a bad conscience and uncertain of forgiveness and salvation. These readers do not need a list of what is required of them; rather, they must understand the gracious provision God has made in Jesus Christ.

Conclusion

Paul began Hebrews by pointing out Christ's superiority to angels, Moses, and Aaron (Hebrews 1–7). After summarizing his discussion in Hebrews 8:1, 2, he turns to the covenant, the sanctuary, and the sacrifice, and from that point on he focuses on Jesus' accomplishments. Paul says the new covenant allows for a special relationship to God and offers the solution to our deepest needs and problems. We are blessed by a new, better covenant, a perfect Sacrifice, and the best possible High Priest and Mediator—Jesus, our Lord.

---

1. Elizabeth Achtemeier, *The Committed Marriage* (Philadelphia: Westminster Press, 1976), 41.
2. Gerhard F. Hasel, *Covenant in Blood* (Nampa, Idaho: Pacific Press, 1982).
3. Ibid., 18.
4. Heb. 8:6, 8, 9, 10. Four of the five references are part of the OT quotation. However, the covenant is implied in other places. Most translations add the word *covenant* in verse 13, although the Greek uses only the adjective *new.*
5. The seven references to *covenant* in Hebrews 9 are found in 9:4, 15, 16, 17, 20.
6. For a short summary of the covenant in Hebrews, see Ellingworth, 413.
7. Quoted in Lane, *Hebrews 1–8,* 204.
8. Hasel, 77, 106.
9. See especially Johnsson, *In Absolute Confidence,* 105.
10. Guthrie, 165, 166, 174.

Jesus and the Sanctuary

In tracing the sanctuary theme through Scripture, one notices that the term *temple (naos)* may assume different meanings. Sometimes it stands for a heathen temple. Most often it refers to God's sanctuary in heaven and His sanctuary on earth. In the New Testament, the "christological" dimension is added: Jesus Himself is the temple (John 2:21). And because of Jesus, those who belong to Him—His church—also comprise the temple, as do individual believers (1 Cor. 3:16; 6:19). This is the "ecclesiological" dimension. Finally, there is the "eschatological" dimension—the end-time dimension, when God and the Lamb replace the temple (Rev. 21:22) and the New Jerusalem becomes the Most Holy Place.

The Meaning of the Sanctuary Understanding

1.	Temple on earth	literal
2.	Temple in heaven	literal
3.	Jesus	christological
4.	The church / believers	ecclesiological
5.	God and the Lamb	eschatological

The epistle of Hebrews focuses on the earthly and heavenly sanctuaries only, developing the relation between them. Consequently, it avoids to some extent the term *naos,* and sticks with words that do not express the additional dimensions (the christological, etc.). Since in this epistle Paul restricted himself to the literal understanding of the sanctuary, we should not spiritualize our interpretation.

I. The Relation Between the Earthly and the Heavenly Sanctuaries

Hebrews considers the earthly sanctuary to be a copy of the real sanctuary, the one in heaven. The focal points of the latter sanctuary are God the Father and especially Jesus Christ.

Although other parts of Hebrews refer to the sanctuary, chapter 9 contains the heaviest concentration of sanctuary terms. This chapter can be divided into two major parts. The first part extends from verse 1 to verse 10. The term *regulations* is found in the first and last verses of this first section, setting its boundaries. Verse 1 introduces the topics of this passage, and the following verses treat these topics in reverse order.

Hebrews 9

I. The worship under the old covenant (Heb. 9:1-10)

1. Introduction: a. regulations for worship and
   b. earthly sanctuary (9:1)
2. Description of the earthly sanctuary (9:2-5; see b)
3. Regulations for worship in the earthly sanctuary (9:6-10; see a)

II. The sacrifice of Jesus and the new covenant (Heb. 9:11-28)

1. Christ's ministry in the heavenly sanctuary (9:11-14)
2. Blood as the basis for Christ's new covenant ministry (9:15-22)
3. Christ's ministry in the heavenly sanctuary (23–28)

The second part of the chapter begins and ends with the word *Christ* (9:11, 28), the name denoting Jesus in this chapter.[1] It is more difficult to outline this second part.

Hebrews uses typology to communicate important truths. In biblical typology, a "type" is a historical person, event, or institution ordained by God to prefigure directly or indirectly a greater reality—the "antitype"[2]—oftentimes in a pattern of prediction and fulfillment. The Greek New Testament uses the words *typos* and *antitypos,* which oftentimes are translated respectively as "type" and "pattern"/"copy." Typology is acted instead of spoken prophecy.

The term *antitype* does not mean someone or something that is opposed to the type.[3] The antitype has the same basic features that the type has; typology stresses continuity. However, the antitype is not an exact representation of the type; they meet only in certain aspects. And the antitype surpasses the type by far.

Romans 5:14 calls Adam a type (*typos*) of Christ. Adam is the type, and Jesus is the antitype. In some respects Adam and Jesus are similar. Both are fathers of humanity. Adam is the father of all humans, and he has transmitted sin and death to all his descendants. Jesus is the father of born-again humans; He has transmitted His righteousness and life to them.

In Hebrews 8:5b; 9:24 the words *pattern* and *copy*—in Greek *typos* and *antitypos*—are used to describe the correspondence between the earthly and the heavenly sanctuaries. (Hebrews differs from other biblical books in that it calls the reality the *typos* and the prefiguring "shadow" the *antitypos.*) The earthly sanctuary is a copy of the original one, the heavenly. Both are real, but the heavenly by far surpasses the earthly. In Hebrews 8:5, Paul quotes Exodus 25:40, stressing the correspondence between the earthly and the heavenly temples.

In Hebrews 8:5; 9:9, 23 the terms *hypodeigma* ("pattern," "copy"), *skia* ("shadow," "foreshadowing"), and *parabolē* ("parable") are used as synonyms of the word *antitypos.* They describe the earthly sanctuary, which is inferior to the heavenly but still corresponds with it.

This typological picture is unique: The heavenly temple existed prior to the earthly; yet in function, i.e., with regard to the ministry performed by Christ, it follows the copy. Furthermore, since the copy prefigures the reality, it is permissible to argue also from the copy to the greater reality. This is evident in Hebrews 9:23. Therefore, we may draw conclusions about the heavenly reality from the structure and service of the earthly tabernacle.

Solomon's temple corresponded with the wilderness tent. Both had a Holy Place and a Most Holy Place. But Solomon's temple surpassed the tabernacle, having many additional rooms and other features. The earthly sanctuary prefigures the heavenly tabernacle, so there must be some correspondence between the two. Since the earthly temple had two major apartments, the heavenly must have no fewer than two major "rooms." In John 14:1-3 Jesus informed us about the many dwelling places in His Father's house. Apparently, He was talking about the heavenly sanctuary, which includes many rooms in addition to the Holy and Most Holy Places.

We have biblical evidence indicating that the heavenly temple has similar basic furnishings to the earthly—which adds to the evidence that, like the earthly, it has two major apartments. Revelation 8:3 depicts heaven's golden altar of incense. Obviously, it is found in the Holy Place. And in Revelation 11:19 we notice the ark of the covenant in the Most Holy Place.

The Lord has allowed us to talk about the heavenly sanctuary in terms of the earthly because there is no other way for us to talk about it. But the heavenly sanctuary cannot be limited to what we can grasp about the earthly. If we deny the existence of a real heavenly sanctuary including at least the features that the earthly sanctuary and its ministry had, we are disregarding biblical typology and spiritualizing away the substance of biblical texts.

II. Terms That Describe the Sanctuary

The Greek terms for the earthly and heavenly sanctuaries are *skēnē* ("tent," "tabernacle") and *hagion/hagia* ("sanctuary," "holy place"). While these terms normally denote the entire sanctuary, sometimes they refer to only a part of it.

"Tent"/"tabernacle" *(skēnē)* is found in Hebrews 8:2, 5; 9:2, 3, 6, 8, 11, 21; 11:9; 13:20. In Hebrews 11:9 *skēnē* denotes Abraham's tents, but everywhere else it points to the sanctuary. The following table shows the different shades of meanings of *skēnē*; the context indicates which meaning is to be preferred. When *skēnē* is applied to the Holy Place or the Most Holy Place, it is clearly modified by additional words.[4] Otherwise it stands for the entire sanctuary.

The Term *skēnē* in Hebrews

1. Abraham's tents	11:9
2. The earthly sanctuary	8:5; 9:8, 21; 13:10
3. The Holy Place ("the first tent") of the earthly sanctuary	9:2, 6
4. The Most Holy Place of the earthly sanctuary ("the tent called the Holy of Holies")	9:3
5. The heavenly sanctuary	8:2; 9:11

"Sanctuary"/"Holy Place" *(to hagion/ta hagia)* is found in Hebrews 8:2; 9:1, 2, 8, 12, 24, 25; 10:19; 13:11. As noted above, the word can also be used as an adjective ("holy"). The texts in which the term does not refer to the sanctuary or any part of it have been excluded from the following comments.[5] Unfortunately, *to hagion/ta hagia* has been translated inconsistently. And the translations have important implications. If, for instance, it is translated as "Most Holy Place" and it is claimed that Jesus had already begun His Most Holy Place ministry in Paul's day, that would mean that the antitypical day of atonement began in the first century A.D. instead of in 1844. This interpretation, then, would collapse the two phases of Jesus' high-priestly ministry into one, seriously distorting the biblical sanctuary doctrine. Let us take a look at how different English translations have rendered the term.

Reference	KJV	RSV	NAB	NASB	NIV
8:2	sanctuary	sanctuary	sanctuary	sanctuary	sanctuary
9:1	sanctuary	sanctuary	sanctuary	sanctuary	sanctuary
9:2	Holy Place	Holy Place	Holy Place	Holy Place	Holy Place
9:8	Holiest of all	sanctuary	sanctuary	Holy Place	Most Holy Place
9:12	Holy Place	Holy Place	sanctuary	Holy Place	Most Holy Place
9:24	Holy Place	sanctuary	sanctuary	Holy Place	sanctuary
9:25	Holy Place	Holy Place	sanctuary	Holy Place	Most Holy Place
10:19	Holiest	sanctuary	sanctuary	Holy Place	Most Holy Place
13:11	sanctuary	sanctuary	sanctuary	Holy Place	Most Holy Place

In Hebrews 9:3—and only here—we encounter the phrase *hagia hagiōn.* This doubling of the word means "the holy of the holy/holies," an unmistakable reference to the Most Holy Place. Since Paul used this special phrase when he wanted to specify the Most Holy Place, the safest course is to translate the simple terms *to hagion* and *ta hagia* as "sanctuary" or—if required by the context—"Holy Place." Chapter 8:2 confirms this translation. In this verse, *ta hagia* is identified with the *skēnē* ("tabernacle"), which clearly refers to the entire sanctuary. "It is reasonable to assume that he [the author of Hebrews] is following that version's [the Septuagint's] common practice of employing *ta hagia* as a descriptive term for the entire sanctuary . . . except in Hebrews 9:2, 3 where the two apartments (holy, Most Holy) are explicitly specified."[6]

The translation of *to hagion/ta hagia* as "sanctuary" includes possible references to the Most Holy Place. But translating these terms as "the Most Holy Place" rules out the broader meaning of the sanctuary as a whole and is too limiting. Hebrews 9:25 alludes to the Day of Atonement. But this reference does not require us to translate the Greek term in that verse as the "Most Holy Place." On the Day of Atonement, the high priest ministered blood in both apartments, which "sanctuary," the broader term, would encompass.[7] Although Hebrews mentions the two apartments of the earthly sanctuary that correspond to the heavenly sanctuary, the apostle's interest is not in the apartments. His point is that Jesus is our High Priest and is ministering in the heavenly sanctuary on our behalf.

We must also keep in mind that God is not limited to the Most Holy Place (see Deut. 23:14). Apparently, some people imagine that Jesus entered the heavenly sanctuary after His ascension but had no access to the Father until 1844 because the Father supposedly resided only in the Most Holy Place and Jesus couldn't go there until He began the second phase of His ministry. That's a mistaken idea. The fact that Jesus didn't begin His special work in the Most Holy Place until 1844 doesn't mean that He couldn't enter that apartment before then. Conversely, Jesus' access to the heavenly sanctuary and its different apartments prior to 1844 doesn't mean that He started the second phase of His ministry before that date.

III. The Character of the Earthly and the Heavenly Sanctuaries

The heavenly sanctuary is the true sanctuary (8:2). God did institute the earthly sanctuary, so though it was symbolic, it was real. However, Paul stressed the contrast three times: The earthly sanctuary was made with hands—in other words, by humans, sinners (8:2; 9:11, 24). The Lord pitched the heavenly tabernacle (8:2).

The function of the earthly sanctuary was limited in effectiveness as well as in time. Its service couldn't solve the sin problem. The shedding of blood there had no lasting effect. The human conscience was not really cleansed (9:9). The earthly sanctuary and its services were just a copy of the genuine sanctuary and its services. Only the blood of Jesus and His ministry as High Priest make a real, lasting difference. Jesus, who has entered the heavenly sanctuary, has "obtained eternal redemption" (9:12, NIV).

However, the apostle didn't ridicule the old sanctuary, although he pointed out its limitations. The new is the fulfillment of the old, not its contradiction.[8] God had His people build the wilderness tabernacle so that He could dwell among them. It was called the tent of meeting. Yet Hebrews notes that barriers still separated God from humans (9:8); sin has blocked our access to God. But Jesus has given us access to God's very presence. We may approach Him boldly and yet reverently. And in the age to come, we will enjoy His immediate presence. The basic intention of the sanctuary is to bring us close to God and provide for our salvation.[9] That salvation comes from the sanctuary, through the Cross and Christ's ministry on our behalf.

IV. The Two-Part Earthly Sanctuary in Hebrews 9

In Hebrews 9:1-10, Paul pointed out the limitations of the Old Testament services before he moved on to the better ministry of Jesus. This passage says the earthly sanctuary had two apartments and two distinct ministries, those of the regular priests and of the high priest.

Hebrews 9:4 seems to place the golden altar inside the Most Holy Place, whereas Exodus 30:1-6 places it in the Holy Place, in front of the second veil. The apostle was not ignorant about the Old Testament sanctuary. The altar of burnt offerings related to the Holy Place—the blood of its sacrifices was ministered in the first apartment. Similarly, the altar of incense related to the Most Holy Place—its smoke penetrated behind the curtain, and God's presence extended out from the throne between the cherubim in the Most Holy Place throughout the sanctuary. "We should also notice that the writer does not say that his altar was 'in' the Most Holy Place, but only that that place 'had' it. . . . He merely says that it belonged to the sanctuary."[10]

Another difficulty is found in Hebrews 9:8. In verse 2 of that chapter the "first tent" *(skēnē)* is the Holy Place of the sanctuary on earth. Verse 8 uses the same phrase, the "first tent." The question is, in verse 8 does this phrase refer only to the first apartment or to the entire earthly sanctuary?

The immediate context (verse 2) would suggest the first apartment when it uses precisely the same expression. Furthermore, verses 11, 12 make sense if the "tent" *(skēnē)* through which Jesus passes in order to enter *ta hagia*—according to this view the Most Holy Place—is the Holy Place and not the entire sanctuary. However, this view militates against our previous conclusion regarding *ta hagia*.

On the other hand, time indicators in verses 8-10 suggest that Paul has switched the perspective from the spatial to the temporal. The "first tent"[11] in verse 8 is not the first apartment of the earthly temple but the entire earthly tabernacle, where ministry was carried out before Jesus began His ministry in the heavenly "sanctuary." "Those who take other views underestimate the facility with which the author [of Hebrews] can glide from one meaning of an expression to another."[12]

V. Jesus and the Heavenly Sanctuary in Hebrews 9

Hebrews 9:11-14 forms a sharp contrast to the paragraph that precedes it. The passage starts with the word *Christ.* Elsewhere in Hebrews only chapters 3:6; 13:8 place Jesus in this emphatic position right at the beginning of a sentence. Paul was saying, "Here is the heart of the matter: Jesus Christ, the sacrifice and the high priest in the heavenly sanctuary."

Verses 24, 25 resemble verses 11, 12. Both passages mention an earthly sanctuary "made with hands." Both speak about a greater reality than the earthly temple. Both stress that Jesus entered there with His own blood. They say that His death was a once-for-all-time sacrifice that does not allow for repetition. But whereas verses 11, 12 stress that Jesus entered the heavenly sanctuary, verses 24, 25 state that Jesus "entered . . . heaven itself." This phrase does not militate against a heavenly sanctuary. Lane suggests: "Christ entered . . . 'into heaven itself,' which is to be defined as the place of God's dynamic presence. . . . Elsewhere in Hebrews the writer uses the plural form . . . 'heavens'; only in v 24 does he make use of the singular to denote the highest heaven in which the true sanctuary as the dwelling place of God is located."[13]

"The heavenly is presented as the ultimate source of meaning for the earthly. . . . The sacrifice of Christ on earth is viewed as taking place on an altar that is in the (earthly) court of the heavenly sanctuary. Christian worshipers have salvation in Christ as they by faith relate to him in the heavenly sanctuary . . . where he intercedes on their behalf."[14]

Conclusion

The earthly sanctuary is a copy of the true, greater tabernacle, which the Lord erected. The heavenly sanctuary gives meaning to the earthly.

The earthly sanctuary contains two apartments: the Holy Place and the Most Holy Place. Although Paul did not specifically stress, in the book of Hebrews, two apartments in the heavenly sanctuary and two phases of ministry, he hinted at the idea through the relation of the earthly to the heavenly and through depicting Jesus not only as priest but also as high priest. He *did* stress as most important that Jesus shed His blood for us as the ultimate, once-and-for-all sacrifice and now serves on our behalf as the true high priest in the true sanctuary.

The sanctuary concept is related to the great controversy theme and the plan of salvation. The sanctuary doctrine describes God's redemptive plan for humanity. But the sanctuary is more than merely an aid to solving the sin problem. Before sin existed on earth, the Garden of Eden was a sanctuary—as will be the New Jerusalem. So, we would be misguided to suggest that the heavenly sanctuary was created as a response to the sin problem. And yet, salvation is dependent on Christ as sacrifice and High Priest in the sanctuary. Through Him we draw close to the Lord of the universe. To Him we surrender our life.

---

1. The heaviest concentration of the name *Christ* in Hebrews is found in chapter 9. On the other hand, *Jesus* is not found in that chapter.

2. See C. T. Fritsch, "Principles of Biblical Typology," *Bibliotheca Sacra* 104 (1947):214, and Richard M. Davidson, "Biblical Interpretation," in *Handbook of Seventh-day Adventist Theology, Commentary Reference Series,* Raoul Dederen, ed. (Hagerstown: Review and Herald, 2000), 12:83, 84.

3. The Greek *anti* normally means "in place of" or "instead of."

4. An adjective or a relative clause is added.

5. For a detailed discussion of the term, see Alwyn P. Salom, "*Ta Hagia* in the Epistle to the Hebrews," in *Issues in the Book of Hebrews,* F. B. Holbrook, ed. (Silver Spring, Md.: Biblical Research Institute, 1989), 219-227.

6. Frank Holbrook, *The Atoning Priesthood of Jesus Christ* (Berrien Springs: ATS Publications, 1996), 23, 24.

7. See Exod. 30:10; Lev. 16:16-19; John I. Durham, *Exodus, Word Biblical Commentary* (Waco: Word Book, Publisher, 1987), 3:399.

8. Morris, 80.

9. See Ex. 25:22; 29:43-46; Rev. 7:15-17; Heb. 4:16; 10:19-23.

10. Morris, 82.

11. "First tent" is sometimes translated "outer tent," which is not a literal translation.

12. Ellingworth, 438.

13. Lane, 248.

14. R. M. Davidson, *Typology in Scripture* (Berrien Springs: Andrews University Press, 1981), 357.

Jesus' Ministry and the Sanctuary

"An old man, walking the beach at dawn, noticed a young man ahead of him picking up starfish and flinging them into the sea. Catching up with the youth, he asked what he was doing. The answer was that the stranded starfish would die if left until the morning sun. 'But the beach goes on for miles, and there are millions of starfish,' countered the old man. 'How can your effort make a difference?' The young man looked at the starfish in his hand and then threw it to safety in the waves. 'It makes a difference to this one,' he said."[1]

Jesus died for us and now serves as high priest in the heavenly sanctuary to save human beings. His ministry is comprehensive enough to save all of us, but unlike the starfish we can resist. If we do, even the ministry of Jesus can't help us, because He won't force us to be saved against our will.

The priests and sanctuary services existed for one purpose: to provide salvation. Hebrews shows how the Old Testament services foreshadowed Christ's ministry. In Hebrews Paul mentions both the daily service of the Old Testament sanctuary ritual and the yearly service. He alludes to the Day of Atonement in several places, though he doesn't develop its typological meaning. He's content to point to Christ as the supreme sacrifice and the supreme priest. For the sake of each of us

Christ laid down His life, worth no less than the universe. He asks of us in return that we live our lives for the sake of one another.

I. The Daily Service in Hebrews

In agreement with the Old Testament, Hebrews distinguishes between ministry in the Holy Place (9:6) and ministry in the Most Holy place (9:7). In the former the priests, serving daily, offered sacrifices and atoned for the sins of the people (Exod. 29:38-42; 30:7, 8). In the latter, once a year the high priest made final atonement for sins and cleansed it from the sanctuary (Ex. 30:10; Leviticus 16). Thus, the two types of services are clearly differentiated. However, both have in common the priestly administration of blood to atone for sins. Sin defiles, but blood acts "as a purging medium."[2]

The daily ministry in the earthly sanctuary is mentioned also in Hebrews 7:26, 27; 10:11, 12; and probably indirectly in 13:10. The term *daily* specifies this ministry. In Hebrews 13:10 the right to eat from the altar reminds us of Leviticus 6 and 10:17, which also speak of the daily service. Part of the cereal offering was eaten by the priests (Lev. 6:14-16). Atonement was made when priests took the blood of the sacrifice into the Holy Place or when they ate some of the meat, which also affected the sanctuary (Lev. 6:26-30).[3]

II. The Day of Atonement and Other Sanctuary Services in Hebrews

Hebrews contains three clear references to the annual Day of Atonement—Hebrews 9:7, 25, 26; 10:1-4. This yearly service may lie behind other sections of the book too, but not indisputably—for instance, in the references to the veils (Heb. 6:19; 10:20). Even Paul's mention of the high priest may point to the Day of Atonement, because it was on that day that the high-priestly office took on particular significance. Admittedly, however, the high priest could minister on other occasions as well.

Hebrews 9:7 refers to the Day of Atonement found in Leviticus 16 and other passages. This annual ceremony was a solemn ritual involving aspects of cleansing and judgment. This verse discusses the Day of

Atonement in the earthly sanctuary only—as does Hebrews 9:25. The latter text stresses that the high priest performs the Day of Atonement service just once a year, but notes that it must be repeated year after year. Hebrews 10:1, 3 refers also to the Day of Atonement in the earthly sanctuary. It highlights again that service's ineffectiveness. Consequently, it is clear that the earthly Day of Atonement doesn't provide the final solution to the sin problem. That solution is Christ's once-and-for-all sacrifice and His ministry. We need the blood of Jesus.[4]

The Day of Atonement includes judgment (see Lev. 23:27-30). Hebrews 10:26-30 deals with judgment. It says the judgment has not been executed yet. Before the execution of the sentence can take place, witnesses have to confirm the guilt of the defendants (10:28, 29). While this judgment passage doesn't establish a direct relation to the Day of Atonement, it alludes to an investigative process.

Hebrews 9:13-22 hints at various ceremonies that were part of the old covenant and notes the different animals used as sacrifices. The mention of sacrifices of goats and bulls and the heifer seems to point to the entire system of sacrifices rather than specifically to the Day of Atonement.[5] Hebrews 9:18-21 refers to the dedication of the sanctuary, a special ceremony. The word translated "to inaugurate" in Hebrews 9:18 (NAB) is crucial. Its noun forms are used in the Septuagint for the dedication of the sanctuary, but not for the Day of Atonement.[6] In Hebrews 9:20, a quotation from Exodus 24:8 is used. Its context is the establishment of the Sinaitic covenant. This covenant involved the law and the sanctuary (Exod. 24:12; 25:8, 9). Moses was instrumental in making this covenant, and it is he who is mentioned in Hebrews 9:18-21. The passage tells what he did to dedicate the earthly sanctuary.

The Most Holy Place was entered on only two occasions: (1) when Moses dedicated the sanctuary and the Levitical priesthood (Exod. 40:1-9; Leviticus 8; Num. 7:1) and (2) on the Day of Atonement (Leviticus 16). Hebrews 10:20 is the only New Testament passage besides 9:18 that uses this word meaning "to inaugurate." As the old covenant and its sanctuary were inaugurated, so Jesus inaugurated the new covenant and its sanctuary and provided access to the throne of grace.

Another fascinating text—Hebrews 9:23—follows the passage on the dedication of the sanctuary. Just as the earthly things—that is, the entire earthly sanctuary[7]—require purification, so do the heavenly things.[8] However, the heavenly require better sacrifices. The preceding context may point us toward the dedication of the heavenly sanctuary, but this is not the whole picture. Hebrews 9:25 includes a reference to the Day of Atonement. The term *katharizō* ("to purify") is found also in Leviticus 16; the sanctuary was purified during the Day of Atonement (Lev. 16:19, 20, 30). This term is found as well in Daniel 8:14. It hints at Christ's second-phase ministry in the heavenly sanctuary. Although Hebrews does not elaborate more on this theme, it affirms not only that there is a sanctuary in heaven but that the sanctuary needs purification through a better sacrifice.

Was purification of the sanctuary completed at the Cross? If this were the case, there would be no need for Christ's heavenly ministry. However, verse 24 has a post-crucifixion dimension. "Now"—in other words, at the time when the apostle wrote the epistle, decades after the Cross—Christ was appearing "in the presence of God for us" (NASB). Verses 27 and 28 have an eschatological dimension, pointing to the judgment and the Second Coming. "The cross event did not cleanse the heavenly sanctuary at the moment of the Savior's death, but it did provide the basis upon which Christ, as man's high priest, could mediate his merits and bring about a total reconciliation of the universe (cf. Eph. 1:10; Col. 1:20) and thus restore the heavenly sanctuary and government of God 'to its rightful state' (Dan. 8:14, RSV)."[9]

Thus, Hebrews 9 presents the daily service (vs. 6), different ceremonies (vs. 13), the dedication of the temple (vss. 18-22), and the Day of Atonement (vss. 7, 25). All of them require better sacrifices, all of which find their fulfillment in the shedding of Jesus' blood, which alone makes forgiveness possible (vs. 22).

III. An Anchor Within the Veil and a New Way Through the Veil

Paul used the Greek word translated "veil" three times in Hebrews—chapters 6:19; 9:3; 10:20 (NASB). The second text deals with the earthly sanctuary and calls the veil separating the Holy Place from the Most

Holy Place "the second veil." This passage is clear. However, the other two do not relate to the earthly sanctuary. Hebrews 10:19, 20 (NASB) says that "we have confidence to enter the holy place by the blood of Jesus, by a new and living way which He inaugurated for us through the veil, that is, His flesh." Is Jesus' flesh the "new and living way" or is His flesh the "veil"?

The first alternative makes Jesus' flesh the way to God. The veil, then, may refer to the heavenly sanctuary. In the second case, "veil" is understood symbolically as representing Jesus' incarnation and death. In this case it would not refer to either the earthly or the heavenly sanctuaries. The opinion of scholars is divided.[10] However one understands this verse, though, the meaning is evident: Through Jesus we have access to God.

The most disputed text is Hebrews 6:19 (NASB), which says our "hope . . . enters within the veil." The question is whether this veil is the one that separates the courtyard from the Holy Place or the one that separates the Holy Place from the Most Holy Place.[11] Many favor the second alternative. Some of them go one step further and claim the text indicates that immediately after Jesus' ascension He entered the Most Holy Place and started the second phase of His high-priestly ministry. Their interpretation invalidates the significance of 1844.

George Rice takes the position that the veil in chapter 6:19 is not specifically the veil to the Most Holy Place. He says this verse has in view the entire sanctuary to which Christ has given us access and in which our hope is anchored. Rice says that the veil in Hebrews 6:19 cannot be associated with the second veil and that the context of chapter 6 does not contain allusions to the Day of Atonement.[12]

Rice has a point when he says that the phrase "within the veil" is found nowhere else in Scripture. Though the wording in Exodus and Leviticus closely resembles this phrase, nevertheless it differs slightly. Hebrews must get a fair reading; one must be careful not to read more into a letter than the author wanted to say.

Others point out that the phrase used in Hebrews 6:19 resembles very closely the Greek of Exodus 26:33 and Leviticus 16:2, 12, 15, which always refers to the Most Holy Place. They conclude that, therefore, the veil of Hebrews 6:19 should be understood as the second veil, and that in this case, the verse refers to the Day of Atonement.[13]

Richard Davidson argues for the second veil.[14] However, he suggests a connection to the dedication of the sanctuary. His starting point is Hebrews 10:19, 20. He proposes that this passage is parallel to Hebrews 6:19, 20 and so can be used to explain it. He says that Christ's flesh in chapter 10:19ff is not the veil. Rather, this verse points to the dedication of the sanctuary; the inauguration motif it contains forms the background for Hebrews 6:19 as well. The passage says that our hope reaches within the Most Holy Place, where Jesus went to inaugurate the sanctuary after His ascension to heaven. The validity of the 1844 message is not affected. One wonders, though, why the apostle talks about the "second veil" in Hebrews 9:3 and not in these other places if he really wanted to point to this particular veil.

Anyway, one must be careful not to overstate the case. To make the phrase "within the veil" central and focus exclusively on it misses the whole point of Hebrews, which is that through Jesus' death and mediation all barriers between God and humanity have been broken down and we now have full access to the Father. "Hope in Christ, their living high priest in God's presence, could be for them 'an anchor of the soul, both sure and steadfast' (vs. 19)."[15] Even with its Day of Atonement imagery, this verse does not prove that the Day of Atonement ministry was fulfilled at the Cross.

IV. The Role of the Day of Atonement in Hebrews

While Hebrews speaks of the heavenly sanctuary and the ministry connected with it, elements of the Adventist sanctuary doctrine seem to be missing. We do not find therein statements that explicitly depict a two-part heavenly sanctuary or a two-phase ministry. This epistle doesn't emphasize the investigative judgment. It gives us no clear time spans—such as those found in Daniel—relating to different phases of Christ's heavenly sanctuary ministry. Therefore, some have concluded that Hebrews contradicts or undermines the Adventist sanctuary doctrine.

However, we have to base our conclusions on what a biblical book teaches, not on what it omits. Matthew did not include the millennium in his end-time scenario (see Matthew 24). That does not mean he denied the thousand years following the Second Coming. If Hebrews doesn't mention the 2,300 evenings and mornings, that doesn't mean the author rejected this prophetic time span. Paul had one crucial message for the Hebrew Christians: "Don't abandon the Lord! Don't fall back!" So, he showed why his hearers and readers should hold on to Jesus. He said Jesus is the better sacrifice and the better high priest, who has instituted a better covenant and serves in a better sanctuary. To make his point, Paul used the parts of the sanctuary message that were helpful to his audience in the current crisis. That he omitted other parts doesn't mean he denied them.[16]

On the other hand, the author of Hebrews confirmed important elements of the sanctuary message. He confirmed that the sacrifice of Christ fulfills and surpasses all Old Testament sacrifices, including those of the Day of Atonement. He confirmed that Jesus conducts a high-priestly ministry in the heavenly sanctuary. He confirmed that the heavenly sanctuary is a real place. He confirmed that the earthly and the heavenly sanctuaries are related and that it is permissible to draw basic conclusions from one regarding the other. He confirmed that the heavenly sanctuary needs purification. He confirmed that there is a future judgment. He confirmed that the sanctuary and its ministry are tied to our salvation.[17]

V. Jesus' Ministry

The book of Hebrews stresses the importance of the death and priestly ministry of Christ. However, it doesn't fully develop all His priestly functions. Priests administered sacrifices (Lev. 1:7-9, 11), trimmed lamps (Exod. 27:20, 21), burned incense (Exod. 30:7, 8), and replaced the showbread (Lev. 24:8, 9). They were involved in health-related issues (Lev. 13:1-3), blessed people (Num. 6:22-27), inquired concerning God's will for individuals (Deut. 33:8; 1 Sam. 14:36-42), and taught the law of God (Deut. 33:10).

During His life on earth, Jesus carried out many of these functions. He cared for the well-being of people. He healed and blessed them. He preached and taught. Although Hebrews does not focus on these aspects, our heavenly High Priest is no less thoughtful, loving, merciful, and caring now that He ministers in heaven. Jesus is Sacrifice, Priest, High Priest, Minister of the true tabernacle, Mediator, and Intercessor (Heb. 7:25; 8:2; 9:15, 25; 10:12, 21).

A priest had to take care of relations between estranged parties—he was a connecting link between God and humanity. "The priestly ministry in connection with the first apartment in both type and antitype is *primarily individual-centered.* It is concerned with reconciling the sinner to God. . . . This priestly activity is thus focused on the doctrinal areas of justification and sanctification. . . . Moreover, these subjects of the first apartment ministry in type are also the concerns of Christ's antitypical ministry in the heavenly sanctuary. Hence, we properly describe His initial priestly service as a *ministry of forgiveness, reconciliation, and restoration.*"[18] The yearly ministry was more corporate-centered and dealt with the final eradication of sin, the cleansing of the sanctuary, the vindication of believers and God, and judgment.

In the Old Testament sanctuary service the priests, as representatives of the worshippers, would go where they couldn't go. The priests had to perform this ministry day after day in the daily service and year after year in the Day of Atonement service. Sinners today do not have to purchase an animal, bring it to a sanctuary, kill it, and find another sinner to mediate that blood for them. Now we look to Jesus' once-for-all sacrifice. Through Him we have access to God at any time, at any place. When we sin, we repent, we confess our sins, and Jesus, standing in the presence of God, intercedes for us. His merits become ours by faith. He applies in our behalf the benefits of His perfect life and death. This is the only means by which sinners can be accepted by God. He also hears our prayers. He knows what we desperately need more than we know ourselves, and He provides what He deems best.

Conclusion

Jesus made a difference in the past, He makes a difference in our lives today, and He will do so in the future. "He Himself has said, 'I will never desert you, nor will I ever forsake you' . . . Jesus Christ is the same yesterday and today and forever" (Heb. 13:5, 8, NASB). What a great high priest we have!

---

1. Craig Brian Larson, ed., *Illustrations for Preaching and Teaching From Leadership Journal* (Grand Rapids: Baker Book House, 1993), 66.

2. Lane, *Hebrews 9–13,* 222.

3. See *The Seventh-day Adventist Bible Commentary,* 1:739.

4. For an in-depth study of this topic, see *Issues in the Book of Hebrews,* Frank B. Holbrook, ed. (Silver Spring: Biblical Research Institute, 1989), especially the article "Day of Atonement Allusions" by William G. Johnsson, 105–120. See also Frank B. Holbrook, *The Atoning Priesthood,* 22-30.

5. See the discussion in chapter 6.

6. Num. 7:10, 11, 84, 88. This is the chapter in Numbers dealing with the dedication of the sanctuary (see Num. 7:1).

7. See Heb. 9:21.

8. The word *things* is not found in the Greek text but is required when an article, pronoun, or adjective neuter plural is used that does not refer to a specific noun. This is the case in Heb. 9:23. Therefore, the vast majority of translations insert the term *things.*

9. "Daniel and Revelation Committee Report," in *Issues in the Book of Hebrews,* 9.

10. Morris, 103, 104, claims that the more natural understanding and the one favored by the grammar is to equate flesh with veil. Lane, *Hebrews 9–13,* 284, supports the other view and suggests that "veil" throughout Hebrews must be understood literally. He does see a strong parallel between 10:19, 20 and 6:19, 20.

11. See, e.g., Johnsson, "Day of Atonement Allusions," 105–120. Cp. Holbrook, *The Atoning Priesthood,* 28–30.

12. George Rice, "Hebrews 6:19: Analysis of Some Assumptions Concerning *Katapetasma,*" in *Issues in the Book of Hebrews,* 229–234.

13. Cp. Roy E. Gane, "Re-Opening *Katapetasma* ('Veil') in Hebrews 6:19,"*Andrews University Seminary Studies* 38 (2000): 5–8; Norman H. Young, " 'Where Jesus Has Gone as a Forerunner on Our Behalf' (Heb. 6:20)," *Andrews University Seminary Studies* 39 (2001): 165–173.

14. Richard M. Davidson, "Christ's Entry 'Within the Veil' in Hebrews 6:19, 20: The Old Testament Background," *Andrews University Seminary Studies* 39 (2001): 175–190.

15. "Daniel and Revelation Committee Report," 7. See especially the context of this statement.

16. See Johnsson, *In Absolute Confidence,* 116.

17. Richard M. Davidson, "In Confirmation of the Sanctuary Message," *Journal of the Adventist Theological Society* 2 (1991):107–108.

18. Holbrook, *The Atoning Priesthood,* 112.

CHAPTER 10

Jesus, Our Sacrifice and Salvation

Blood evokes different reactions. Some people faint when they see blood. Others think it is a marvelous substance and call it the stream of life. Still others are afraid of blood because they fear they may get infected. Indeed, on the one hand, blood reminds us of diseases, accidents, wars, and murders. On the other, blood donors save other people's lives.

Blood plays an important role in Scripture. It is mentioned in the Bible's first pages. The slaughter of one or more animals is implied when God provided skins to clothe Adam and Eve (Genesis 3). Thus, the first "sacrifice" took place, and blood was spilled. Blood played an important role in the sanctuary system. The blood of animals was shed in the courtyard of the earthly sanctuary, and through its administration people were symbolically freed from sin and eternal death.

Blood was also featured in other contexts. In Genesis 4 we encounter the first murder, and Abel's blood cries for vengeance (verse 10). Blood is mentioned in the context of wars (1 Chron. 28:3). In the book of Revelation the color red may point to bloodshed (Rev. 6:4; 12:3). And blood is related to diseases: for example, Jesus healed the woman who suffered from hemorrhage (Matt. 9:20-22). In each case blood has to do with life: either life is taken when blood is shed or life is gained because of restoration from sickness or because a substitutionary sacrifice has been made for humankind's sin.

The most important thing blood represents in Scripture is salvation through the atoning sacrifice, the substitutionary death, of Jesus. All other sacrifices were ceremonies that could not save but merely painted a picture of how salvation would be achieved. Jesus laid down His life voluntarily. His supreme sacrifice is the only means to salvation. All other attempts to achieve salvation are doomed to fail.

I. The Centrality of Blood

Hebrews uses the Greek term for "blood" twenty-one times.[1] No other New Testament book uses the term as often. (Revelation is the only book that comes close, using the word nineteen times.)

In Hebrews the term is linked to humans twice (2:14; 12:4), although the first text also applies to Christ. Humans are made of flesh

Christ's Blood in Hebrews

Heb. 9:12, NASB	-	"Through His own blood, He entered the holy place once for all, having obtained eternal redemption."
Heb. 9:14, NASB	-	"How much more will the blood of Christ . . . cleanse your conscience from dead works to serve the living God?"
Heb. 10:19, NASB	-	"We have confidence to enter the holy place by the blood of Jesus."
Heb. 10:29, NASB	-	This verse speaks of the severe punishment of the one "who . . . has regarded as unclean the blood of the covenant by which he was sanctified?"
Heb. 12:24, NASB	-	"The sprinkled blood . . . speaks more graciously than the blood of Abel."
Heb. 13:12, NASB	-	"So Jesus also suffered outside the gate in order to sanctify the people through his own blood."
Heb. 13:24, NASB	-	"The blood of the eternal covenant . . ."

and blood. Jesus took on the same nature; therefore, He was able to lay down His life and shed His blood. Twelve times *blood* designates the blood of animals—particularly, animal sacrifices. These references form the background against which Paul pictures the better sacrifice and the more powerful blood of Jesus. And seven times in Hebrews the word *blood* refers to the blood of Jesus.

Although other New Testament books make extraordinary statements about Christ and His blood,[2] only Hebrews extensively compares the blood of sacrificial animals with His blood. Chapter 9 contains the most occurrences of the term *blood*.[3] And verse 22 of that chapter contains a unique term that in English must be expressed by three words: "shedding of blood." This term, found nowhere else in Scripture, must be added to the references to *blood* already mentioned.

Why is blood so important? Both the old covenant and the new covenant were ratified by blood. Blood made them effective. In Hebrews 9 "the blood of the covenant" refers to the old covenant; and in Hebrews 10–13 it refers to the blood of the new covenant. And with the new covenant come God's outstanding promises.

Hebrews 9:7, 18, 22 all contain the phrases "without blood"/"shedding of blood." The high priest of the old system could not enter the Most Holy Place without blood. The old covenant was not inaugurated without blood. There is no forgiveness of sins without shedding of blood.

Hebrews 9:7-14, 25 contrasts the application of animal blood with the application of the blood of Jesus, thus showing the limits of the old system. Verses 18-21 emphasize the importance of blood with regard to the old covenant and the inauguration of the Old Testament sanctuary. And finally, verse 22 states the basic principle: "Without the shedding of blood there is no forgiveness of sins." So, then, we need a better sacrifice than animals. Christ's blood alone has the power to cleanse from sin.

II. The Effects of Christ's Shed Blood

In the Old Testament, blood is not only a cleansing agent; it may also defile (see Lev. 6:24-30). According to Hebrews, Jesus suffered terribly when He shed His blood (2:18; 5:8; 9:26; 13:12). Nevertheless, the epistle refers to Christ's blood only in positive terms.

The blood of Jesus is very effective. It brings about (1) eternal redemption (9:12), (2) cleansing (9:14), (3) forgiveness (9:22), (4) access to the sanctuary in heaven (10:19), and (5) sanctification (13:12).[4] In addition to what it does for us, Christ's blood cleanses heavenly things (9:23). And in chapter 13:20, His resurrection is linked to His blood.

Hebrews 10:29 has a somewhat negative aspect. But it is not the blood of Jesus that is negative. His blood has a purifying effect. It cleanses the sinner and the sanctuary (see Heb. 9:14, 23) and brings salvation. While the blood of Jesus is positive, though, it may have negative as well as positive effects. Those who accept the blood of Jesus are saved. Those who reject it have to expect condemnation.

III. The Sacrifice of Christ

While the concept of blood dominates Hebrews 9, the terms *sacrifice, offering,* and *to offer* appear most frequently in chapter 10; specifically, sixteen times.

Terms	Occurrences in Hebrews	Occurrences in Hebrews 10
Sacrifice	15[5]	6
Offering	5[6]	5
To offer	18[7]	5
Burnt offering	2[8]	2
Sin offering	3[9]	2

Obviously, then, Hebrews 10 strongly emphasizes sacrifices and offerings, including the act of presenting them.

The first part of Hebrews 10 discusses the inadequacy of the sacrifices of the old covenant. Later in the chapter Paul contrasts Jesus' once-and-for-all sacrifice with the services in the old tabernacle (10:10-18). Lane suggests the following outline:[10]

Hebrews 10:1-18

A The inadequacy of the provisions of the law for repeated sacrifices (10:1-4)
  B Repeated sacrifices superseded by the sacrifice of Christ (10:5-10)
  B' The Levitical priests superseded by the priest Christ (10:11-14)
A' The adequacy of the provisions of the new covenant (10:15-18)

What does the book of Hebrews teach us about Christ's sacrifice?

1. Jesus offered Himself as a sacrifice. Although in some places it is said that He was offered (9:28), the larger number of texts perceive that He took the initiative.[11] Some of these texts also say that Jesus voluntarily accepted humiliation, suffering, and death.[12]

2. Jesus' sacrifice made possible the forgiveness, sanctification, and perfection of people (10:10, 14, 18).

3. Jesus died for sinners. He took our place to make our salvation possible. Today, many people feel uncomfortable with calling Jesus a substitutionary sacrifice for our sins. But people have felt that discomfort since Bible times; Paul wrote, "The message of the cross is foolishness to those who are perishing" (1 Cor. 1:18, NKJV).

People want to believe that we have within ourselves the potential to improve morally, to save ourselves, to reach an almost divine form of existence—or at least that we can pay part of the price for our salvation. We'd rather believe that than admit the total depravity and helplessness of humanity. And it seems easier to believe that God could forgive our sins without requiring the death of His Son than to accept the necessity of His laying down His life in our stead. However, Hebrews teaches that Jesus was without sin (4:15). Thus, when He died as a sacrifice, He did not die for His own sins, but "to make propitiation for the sins of the people" (2:17, NASB). Clearly, then, the Bible teaches Christ's substitutionary sacrifice on our behalf.[13]

4. The terms one, once for all, *and* for all time *(Heb. 9:24-28; 10:10-14) are used to describe Christ's all-sufficient sacrifice.* This invaluable sacrifice is unrepeatable because it was offered once for all. All attempts to repeat it in one way or the other reject its value and undo its effectiveness. A sacrifice of Christ that must be repeated would not surpass the Old Testament system. Such a concept undermines God's plan of salvation and denies Christ's superiority.

IV. The Concept of Purification

The Bible uses a variety of images and terms such as *justification, redemption, atonement, reconciliation, ransom,* and being *in Christ* to describe God's saving activity. With the exception of *redemption* (Heb. 9:12, 15) most of them do not appear in Hebrews. However, Paul did use a similar term, *purification,* in Hebrews.

Justification pictures a legal process in which someone is declared just. *Redemption* pictures something or someone being bought back. *Forgiveness* implies the cancellation of a debt. *Reconciliation* and *atonement* denote the process by which an estranged relationship is healed. *Sanctification* not only points to a process that begins after people are justified but also includes the aspect of salvation, because those who believe in Christ have become saints. *Purification* alludes to the removal of uncleanness and defilement. All these metaphors portray aspects of salvation. They don't contradict one another; they are complementary.

In Hebrews, Paul depicts humanity as in need of purification. Terms from the word family that mean "to cleanse/to purify" are found in chapters 1:3; 9:13, 14, 22, 23; 10:2, 22. The concept occurs first in the prologue of Hebrews, setting the tone for the rest of the epistle: Jesus has made purification of sins. Hebrews 9:14 tells us that our conscience must be purified; the old system could not do that (10:1, 2). Not only humans but also heavenly things require cleansing (9:23); only the blood of Jesus can provide the ultimate cleansing (9:14, 22; 10:22). "By His atonement Christ accomplished both the cleansing of sin in general . . . and the cleansing of the individual from sin. This latter work, also made possible by the cross, is still in progress and will not be finished till the last soul is saved."[14]

The concept of purification stresses what Jesus has done for us and how we from now on should live. Those who have been purified are called to avoid defilement. The apostle warns against the "root of bitterness" that may come up and defile many (12:15). Believers are to hold the marriage bed in honor, to keep it undefiled (13:4).

In the New Testament, defilement and purity involve sexuality (Heb. 13:4), speech (Matt. 15:18), motives (Phil. 1:17), thought processes (1 Tim. 1:5), doctrine (Titus 2:7), worship/religion (James 1:27), and wisdom (James 3:17). Jesus spoke about " 'evil thoughts, murder, adultery, fornication, theft, false witness, slander' " that defile us (Matt. 15:19, 20). Those who have been purified should rejoice, because what they never would have been able to accomplish has been done for them. Those who have been purified should live in purity, shunning defilement.

V. Salvation in Hebrews

The words *salvation* and *to save* are found throughout the epistle from chapter 1 to chapter 11. According to Hebrews 5:7, God was able to save Jesus. Now He is the Author and the Source of our salvation (2:10; 5:9, NASB), and He will appear a second time for salvation (9:28). Thus, Hebrews pictures both Father and Son as saviors. This corresponds with the rest of the New Testament.[15] Jesus is one with the Father.

What does Hebrews say about how humans are saved? Chapter 11:7 mentions the example of Noah. In faith he built the ark that led to his own and his family's salvation. According to chapter 10:38, 39, which uses a synonym for "to save," salvation is by faith—which reminds us of Paul's discussion of the same subject in his letter to the Romans.[16] According to chapter 7:25, those who draw close to God through Jesus Christ are saved. Jesus is not only the Author, the Originator, and Pioneer of our salvation (2:10) but also the Author and Perfecter of our faith (12:2). By faith we are saved. Everything we need for faith, salvation, and assurance comes from Him. Our part is to cling to Him in faith. Those who have faith don't shrink back.

"Christ suffered in order that through faith in Him our sins might be pardoned. He became man's substitute and surety, Himself taking the punishment, though all undeserving, that we who deserved it might be free, and return to our allegiance to God. . . . He is our only hope of salvation. . . . Man repents, becomes contrite in heart, believes in Christ as His atoning sacrifice, and realizes that God is reconciled to him."[17]

Ephesians 2:5, 8 describes salvation as a present reality—as does Hebrews 10:14, by using the words *perfected* and *sanctified.* However, some passages in Hebrews picture it as a future event (1:14; 9:28). So, salvation is both present and yet still future. Although we live with the assurance of our salvation here and now and know salvation as a present reality, we will experience its fullness only at Christ's second coming. Salvation has eternal value and consequences (5:9). Therefore, we should not "neglect so great a salvation" (2:3, NASB) as that brought about by Jesus' sacrifice.

Conclusion

Someone said, "If our greatest need had been information, God would have sent us an educator. If our greatest need had been technology, God would have sent us a scientist. If our greatest need had been money, God would have sent us an economist. If our greatest need had been pleasure, God would have sent us an entertainer. But our greatest need was forgiveness, so God sent us a Savior." We thank Jesus from all our heart for being our Sacrifice, our personal Savior, and our Lord.

---

1. Heb. 2:14, 9:7, 12, 13, 14, 18, 19, 20, 21, 22, 25; 10:4, 19, 29; 11:28; 12:4, 24; 13:11, 12, 20.
2. See, e.g., Rom. 3:25; 5:9; 1 Cor. 11:25; Eph. 1:7; 2:13; Col. 1:20; 1 Peter 1:2, 19; Rev. 1:5; 5:9; 7:14; 12:11.
3. See Ellingworth, 445.
4. See Johnsson, *In Absolute Confidence,* 112, 114.
5. Heb. 5:1; 7:27; 8:3; 9:9, 23, 26; 10:1, 5, 8, 11, 12, 26; 11:4; 13:15, 16.
6. Heb. 10:5, 8, 10, 14, 18.
7. Heb. 5:1, 3, 7; 8:3, 4; 9:7, 9, 14, 25, 28; 10:1, 2, 8, 11, 12; 11:4, 17. The word is also used five times in Hebrews 9. The Greek verb is found in one other place—namely, 12:7; however, with another meaning.
8. Heb. 10:6, 8.
9. Heb. 10:6, 8; 13:11.
10. Lane, *Hebrews 9–13,* 258. See also Vanhoye, *Structure and Message,* 40.
11. See also 7:27; 9:14, 25, 26; 10:12.
12. In the Gospel of John, Jesus' suffering and death are understood as His glorification (e.g., John 7:39); Jesus is lifted up (e.g., John 8:28). The different perspectives of the NT authors supplement each use and draw a magnificent picture of Jesus' sacrifice and love.
13. See Heb. 2:9; 9:28; 10:12; Rom. 5:6-9; 2 Cor. 5:21; Isa. 53:4-6.
14. Nichol, 7:397.
15. See, e.g., Luke 1:47; 2:11; 1 Tim. 1:1; 2 Tim. 1:2; Titus 1:3, 4; 3:4, 6.
16. See, e.g., Rom. 1:17; 5:9, 10; 9:27; 10:9, 13. However, faith is defined somewhat differently in some places in Hebrews.
17. Ellen G. White, *Fundamentals of Christian Education* (Nashville, Tenn.: Southern Publishing Association, 1923), 370.

CHAPTER 11

Jesus, Our Assurance

Most people want as much certainty as they can get in life. Before students decide to attend a particular college or university, they want to know what the program is all about, how much money they'll have to spend, and the school's reputation. Employees look for job security and good pay. Business owners do all they can to make their business flourish. Investors search for investments that promise a good return. Husbands and wives look for evidence that their spouses still love them and will remain faithful even in difficult times. The ill want to learn all they can about their disease, helpful treatments, and the possibility of recovery. In the important aspects of life we want certainty.

What about our relationship to God? Can we afford to live without assurance regarding our salvation?

Those to whom Paul wrote the Epistle to the Hebrews apparently had questions about the Christian life, about forgiveness and cleansing from sin. They needed confidence. The apostle stressed that God offers assurance to believers.

I. Our Status as Followers of Christ

Genuine assurance does not rest on warm feelings that we produce. Feelings are an important part of our life, yet sometimes they deceive.

God's promises are true whatever our feelings. It is faith that counts. For instance, if we fulfill the conditions, God forgives us independently of how guilty we may feel. We need a better, more objective foundation for our salvation than our feelings—namely, Jesus, the Son of God, who died in our stead and who is our King, our Brother, and our High Priest (Heb. 4:14-16).

Our assurance rests not only on the cross of Jesus and His high-priestly ministry but also on His very nature and character. Hebrews 1:10-12 describes Jesus as the one who remains constant, and chapter 13:8 reinforces this concept. Because Jesus is unchangeable, we can have confidence. He will not care for us today and then forget us tomorrow. Hebrews 6:17, 18 speaks of "the unchangeableness of His purpose" and says that "it is impossible for God to lie" so that "we . . . have strong encouragement . . . in laying hold of the hope set before us" (NASB).

Because Jesus has "made purification of sins" (1:3, NASB) and has "obtained eternal redemption" (9:12, NASB), His followers have become "partakers of a heavenly calling" (3:1, NASB), "partakers of Christ" (3:14, NASB), and "partakers of the Holy Spirit" (6:5, NASB). They have "been enlightened" and "have tasted of the heavenly gift" (6:4, NASB). They have been called and so receive "the promise of the eternal inheritance" (9:15). They are "sanctified" (10:10), "perfected" (10:14), with "hearts sprinkled clean" (10:22, NASB) and "washed" (10:22, NASB), and they know that they have "a better possession" (10:34, NASB). Because of what God has done for them, they know that He accepts them and, through Jesus, has given them a new life. So, they have assurance and may approach God boldly.

Evangelical Christians correctly stress the assurance of salvation enjoyed by those who, by faith, have accepted Christ as Savior and Lord. However, some of them take this concept too far, claiming "once saved, always saved." Neither Hebrews nor any other part of Scripture supports this doctrine. Hebrews 3:14 contains an element of conditionality: "*if* we hold fast the beginning of our assurance firm until the end" (NASB, italics added). So does Hebrews 6:4-6. However, the rejection of the motto "once saved, always saved" does not militate against assurance.

Does the sanctuary build assurance in any way? Yes.[1] The various terms describing our salvation are to a large degree sanctuary terms. Johnsson asserts: "Christians are holy, sanctified, perfected, cleansed, purified—all terms associated with the sanctuary and its services. They *are* God's people, even now. Now they are 'clean,' now have access to God, now have consciences purged, now have Jesus as Heavenly High Priest."[2]

The assurance of being saved influences our lifestyle and our witnessing and comforts us during the last hours of our life. It helps us to have a healthy relationship with God. It frees us from the pressure of trying to accomplish our own salvation. The love, gratitude, and trust in God that flow from this assurance permeate our life and result in truly good works. The assurance of being saved also helps us to have healthy relations to our fellow human beings. Since we are already saved, we can minister to them unselfishly. And the certainty of being saved helps us to enjoy personal health of mind and soul.

II. Our Assurance for Today

So far we have surveyed statements that describe the status of those who belong to Christ. Most of these descriptions use verb forms in the past tense. Some people's consciences trouble them terribly because of their sins of the past. God offers a solution—He will clear our record if we will allow Him to. We can still remember our sins when they've been forgiven,[3] but they've been compensated for. So, we can have confidence—assurance—regarding the past.

What about today? Some verses employ verbs in the present tense and spell out Christ's present ministry on our behalf: (1) Jesus takes care of people and comes "to the aid of those who are tempted" (Heb. 2:16, 18, NASB). (2) He can "sympathize with our weaknesses" (4:15, NASB), and He "can deal gently with the ignorant and misguided" (5:2, NASB). (3) He intervenes for His brothers and sisters (7:25).

These verses speak to our present-day life. The terms translated "to sympathize" and "to deal gently" are derived from the same Greek root *(paschō),* differing only in their prefixes.[4] The English words *passion* and *suffering* stem from this verb, which means "to suffer," "to entertain certain feelings." Hebrews uses it four times when speaking of Christ's suffering.[5] The composite terms in Hebrews 4:15; 5:2 in which we are interested may also bear the nuance of suffering.

Sympatheō corresponds to the English term *to sympathize* and means "to feel sympathy for," "to be compassionate toward." A more literal rendering would be "to suffer with someone." This word occurs in only two places in the New Testament: Hebrews 4:15; 10:34. Jesus is compassionate toward us and suffers with us. Likewise, as followers of Christ, the recipients of the Epistle to the Hebrews "showed sympathy to/shared the sufferings with the prisoners."

The term *metriopatheō,* used in Hebrews 5:2, can be translated as "to bear reasonably with someone" and "to be gentle with someone." Because Jesus suffered, He can deal with us gently. He understands us, empathizes with us, and does what is most helpful for us. Therefore, we can be confident.

Christians today enjoy blessings in addition to Jesus' sympathy, intercession, and help. These blessings include strong encouragement, a hope that is like an anchor "sure and steadfast" (6:18-20)—indeed, "a better hope . . . through which we draw near to God" (7:19), and God's instruction and discipline (12:10, 11). The first two passages are very reassuring. Both talk about hope. And although hope normally relates to the future, the "better hope" of chapter 7:19 allows us to draw near to God today.

Hebrews 12:10, 11, on the other hand, sounds negative. The context says the Christian walk includes suffering—enduring evil. Many people today won't tolerate suffering. They anesthetize physical, mental, or emotional pain by plunging into a life of pleasure-seeking. But taking up one's cross—tolerating pain and suffering—is a natural ingredient of the life of Christ's disciples (see Matt. 16:24; Phil. 1:29; 2:17, 18; 1 Peter 4:12, 13). The author of Hebrews perceives the endurance of suffering, hardship, and the battle against sin as means of education and even as signs that God loves us (Heb. 12:6).

It is crucial that we learn to enjoy the blessings bestowed upon us day by day and to view problems from the perspective of God's care through every moment of our lives. Remembering that He uses life's experiences to educate us can fill us with confidence in Him.

III. Our Confidence With Regard to the Future

Trustworthy promises provide assurance for the future. And Hebrews contains a number of such promises: divine rest (4:3), the law written in our hearts and God being our personal God, knowledge of the Lord, forgiveness of sins (8:10, 12; 10:16, 17), Jesus' second coming for our final salvation (9:28), eventual perfection (11:40), reception of an unshakable kingdom (12:28), and the assurance that God will not desert us (13:5, 6).

The "something better" of chapter 11:40 describes what has been achieved by Christ's first coming; however, "the thought reaches ahead to the time of consummation when the sum total of God's people will be complete."[6] And in chapter 12:28, the "present tense of the participle emphasizes that Christians are now in the process of receiving this gift and that this process will continue into the future. . . . It is the prospect of the ultimate enjoyment of the gift in its fullness that provides the motivation for the exhortation to thanksgiving."[7]

The term *promise* occurs fourteen times in Hebrews.[8] We hear about God's promise to Abraham (6:15; 7:6; 11:9, 13, 17), the promise of rest (4:1), "the promised eternal inheritance" (9:15), and the promise of the second coming of Christ and final salvation (10:36-39).

It may be confusing to read that the pioneers of faith *have* obtained and yet have *not* obtained the promises (11:13, 33, 39). But some promises are given for this present age, while others are for the future. Here we see again the tension between the already and the not-yet found so often in Scripture.[9]

Let us in confidence take hold of what God has provided for us today and let us cling to His promises of an extraordinary future. God is faithful. Soon He will establish His kingdom of glory and will bring about the consummation for which we long.

IV. Terms Describing Assurance and Surety

In Hebrews, Paul used a number of Greek nouns with different shades of meaning—such as "conviction," "certainty," "boldness," "confidence," and "full assurance"—in discussing the topic of assurance. Additonally, a verb and adjective speak of surety. However, assurance is not limited to these terms.

Hebrews 6:19 speaks of hope as an anchor. The word *anchor* has nuances of reliability, but Paul added "sure" and "steadfast" for extra emphasis. And in chapter 13:6, he wrote that it is good to know that our Lord is our Helper; we can affirm this promise "with confidence."

Hebrews contains various nouns related to assurance and confidence. These nouns fit into four categories. The first one stresses the fact that we may draw close to God with confidence (4:16; 10:19, 22); we have access to the throne of grace in the heavenly sanctuary. Both Hebrews 4:16 and 10:22 contain imperatives that exhort us to use our privileges. The second group connects assurance and hope (6:11). It calls us to take seriously "the full assurance of hope until the end." The third group links assurance and faith (10:22; 11:1). And the last category calls us to hold fast our confidence, warning us not to throw away our assurance (3:6, 14; 10:35).

All of us experience losses of various kinds: financial loss, loss of influence, loss of employment, loss of friends and family, and loss of spouses due to death or divorce. We encounter diseases, death, disaster, and destruction of our environment. We experience persecution, difficulties with others, ostracism, doubt, and the power of sin. So, questions and doubts may arise: "Why does God allow this? Why doesn't He intervene?" Just as the recipients of Hebrews were in danger of losing their confidence and joy at being children of God, so may we. We're tempted to focus on our problems instead of on God's grace.

Assurance is a delicate gift that we must treasure. We must maintain our relationship with God, and the boldness and confidence that flow from it.

V. Faith and Assurance

Terms from the Greek word family *pist-* appear forty-one times in Hebrews. Unfortunately, English uses terms from a couple different word families to translate the Greek terms, translating the noun as "faith" or "faithfulness" but the verb as "to believe." This distinction in English hides the relationship of the terms.

This word family appears in clusters in Hebrews beginning in chapter 2:17. The next two chapters, Hebrews 3 and 4, focus on faith and rest. Another cluster appears in chapter 6, and the most extensive one runs from the end of chapter 10 through chapter 11, which discusses the heroes of faith.

Hebrews 2:17; 3:2, 5; 4:2, 3 mention faithful Moses and Jesus, rebuke a lack of faith,[10] and explain the benefits of having faith. Chapters 3:6, 14; 4:16 introduce the concept of assurance, as does chapter 6:1, 11, 12, 19, which also mentions hope, God's promises, and the sure anchor. So, faith is closely related to assurance. And Hebrews 4 contains a call to decide and to believe.

Paul pictures faith as practical. On one hand, it leads to assurance and provides hope. On the other, it has to do with the conduct of life and faithfulness. Hebrews 3:18, 19 indicates that Paul considered the terms *disobedience* and *unbelief* interchangeable. To have the full assurance of faith means to live by faith and do the will of God.

We see faith and assurance linked again in chapter 10:19, 22, 23. Then Paul warns his readers not to throw away their confidence, for those who persevere will receive the promise, which is particularly the second coming of Jesus and final salvation (10:35-39). How can they persevere? By faith! Hebrews 11:1 stresses that faith is seeing the unseen. It focuses on God (11:6), and it endures as the heroes of faith have endured. "Faith is an *assurance of the invisible world that perseveres to the end. . . .* Faith in Hebrews is close to *faithfulness.*"[11]

The term *faith* occurs twenty-four times in Hebrews 11. The chapter begins and ends with faith—by which, it says, human beings received God's approval (vss. 1, 2, 39).[12] Here is a brief outline of the chapter:

Hebrews 11

I. Definition of Faith and the Audience ("by faith" / *pistei;* 1 time) (1-3)

II. Examples of Faith

1. *Ten Extensive Examples* ("by faith" / *pistei;* 17 times) (4-31)
   - Abel, Enoch, Noah
   - Abraham and Sarah, Isaac, Jacob, Joseph
   - Moses' parents and Moses, possibly Israel under
   - Moses and Joshua, Rahab
2. *Less Elaborate Examples* (32-34)
   - A list of seven (six persons and one group: Gideon, Barak, Samson, Jephthah, David, Samuel, and the prophets)
   - Nine actions ("by faith" / *dia pisteōs;* 1 time)
3. *Unnamed Heroes of Faith and Their Fate* (35-38)

III. Summary and the Audience ("by faith" / *dia tēs pisteōs;* 1 time) (39-40)

The chapter proceeds chronologically, and there is some "alternation of example and comment."[13] It portrays the patriarchs who lived before the Flood, Abraham and his descendants, Moses and the Exodus, judges, kings, and prophets, and then the unnamed heroes. All, he says, were waiting for a better homeland and the heavenly city, which is still to come. So, Hebrews 11 shows us how important faith is and what it is all about.

1. Faith is related to assurance. The very first verses of Hebrews 11 emphasize this concept. Faith and assurance have to do with things seen and unseen—that is, with the past, the present, and the future. Faith accepts that God created the world in the past (11:3). As to the present, faith accepts the existence of God (11:6). Moses "endured, as seeing Him who is unseen" (11:27, NASB). And faith accepts that God will bring the promised reward, which includes the city of God and the "better country" (11:6, 10, 16). Some of the heroes of faith are great examples of the assurance that faith brings; see Noah,[14] Moses, David, and the prophets.

2. Faith and perseverance or endurance go together. Again, Moses is an outstanding example of faith that endures (11:25-27). And while the end of Hebrews 10 leads into chapter 11's focus on faith through assurance, chapter 11's conclusion on faith leads into chapter 12's theme: endurance. Chapter 11 ends with the unnamed heroes of faith who endured (vss. 35-39), and then chapter 12 depicts Jesus as the prime example of endurance. Because He endured, we are also called to endure (12:1-7).

3. Faith means faithfulness, obedience, and action. See the examples of Abel, Noah, Abraham, Moses, and Daniel and his friends.

4. Faith also has to do with trust. The term *to please* occurs in Hebrews 11:5: Enoch pleased God. How? By trusting Him.

How can we strengthen our faith? (1) By praying for it (Luke 17:5) and asking others to pray for us, (2) by choosing to believe in God and to trust Him (Mark 11:22; John 20:27), (3) by doing God's will regardless of the circumstances and experiencing God's interventions, (4) by sharing our faith and serving others, (5) by listening to fellow believers, reading biographies of modern heroes of faith, and participating in worship services, and (6) by studying God's Word and the life of Jesus Christ.

Conclusion

The foundation of our assurance lies in the sanctuary—more precisely, in Jesus our Sacrifice and heavenly High Priest. "The Sacrifice of Christ assures Christians of two great facts: First, the Act *has been done* that solves the sin problem. . . . Nothing we might do can add to that or diminish from it. Calvary gives us absolute confidence of the putting away of sins. Second, Calvary assures us of our full access to the presence of God. . . . The gates of the temple stand flung open. All who believe may enter—not cringing, but boldly."[15]

"We have the assurance of a Saviour who has come. . . . We have had presented to us . . . the righteousness of Christ, justification by faith, the exceeding great and precious promises of God in his word, free access to the Father by Jesus Christ, the comforts of the Holy Spirit, and the well-grounded assurance of eternal life in the kingdom of God."[16]

By faith we take hold of Christ's achievements and God's promises. This assurance allows us to have a better quality of life and to stretch toward a goal that transcends our present life.

---

1. See, e.g., Heb. 4:14-16.
2. Johnsson, *In Absolute Confidence,* 155.
3. See 1 Tim. 2:15.
4. The Greek term is *paschō*. The present infinite of *paschō* is *pathein,* which better shows the affinity to the words *sumpatheō* and *metriopatheō*.
5. Heb. 2:18; 5:8; 9:26; 13:12.
6. Guthrie, 247.
7. Lane, *Hebrews 9–13,* 484.
8. Heb 4:1; 6:12, 15, 17; 7:6; 8:6; 9:15; 10:36; 11:9, 13, 17, 33, 39. The word occurs most frequently in Heb. 6; 11.
9. See 1 John 3:1.
10. See also Heb. 3:12, 19.
11. Johnsson, *In Absolute Confidence,* 142, 143.
12. See Lane, *Hebrews 9–13,* 320.
13. Ellingworth, 561.
14. Cp. "things not seen" in verses 1, 7.
15. Johnsson, *In Absolute Confidence,* 118.
16. Ellen G. White, *Review and Herald,* January 17, 1899.

CHAPTER 12

Jesus and the Christian Walk

Some countries allow their citizens to maintain double or even multiple citizenships. One may, for example, possess an American passport and a Swiss passport. Passport holders are expected to uphold the value system of their nation, to not dishonor it, and to live by its rules and regulations. Christians hold at least dual citizenship. We are citizens of one or more countries of this world, but our most important citizenship is in heaven. So, we are representatives in this world of the heavenly kingdom. Consequently, there shouldn't be any barriers between members of the church. Not only do we share the same basic theology and task, but we also subscribe to the same basic ethics and lifestyle.

After having presented the heroes of faith in chapter 11, the author of Hebrews draws a conclusion: The privileges that we enjoy should lead to a lifestyle that fits our high calling. The fact that Christ offered the supreme sacrifice for us, that He continues to serve us as the high priest of the heavenly sanctuary, that we are citizens of His kingdom, and that a bright future awaits us, should motivate us to live a holy life, following Jesus' example (see Heb. 12:1, 2a).

I. Christians on the Move

In the Epistle to the Hebrews Paul portrays the people of God as a group of pilgrims traveling to their eternal home. While they live on this earth and are involved in earthly matters, they are primarily citizens of heaven and are on the move to the heavenly city.[1]

Pilgrims are people who have left their home and sometimes even their country. They have broken away—at least temporarily—from their normal activities and their families and friends. They have begun a journey to a sacred place or have left a place of persecution and danger in order to find a new home and a place of peace and rest. Pilgrims have a clear goal and are willing to sacrifice time and money and to endure hardships to reach it.

Oftentimes, pilgrimages are undertaken to gain the favor of a deity, to do penance and receive purification from sins, to show thankfulness, and/or to worship. So, unfortunately, most pilgrimages involve an unbiblical understanding of how one attains salvation.

Hebrews 11–13 contains the pilgrim motif.[2] Abraham is the prototype of a pilgrim. He left his fatherland and after an extensive journey reached the promised land.[3] But even in the promised land he remained an alien and lived in tents. Palestine was not his final goal; he was longing for the heavenly country, the heavenly city. Moses also was a pilgrim who focused on this noble goal, forsaking Egypt and a splendid career.

Whereas Hebrews 12:1 uses the image of Christians running a race to show that we are not at home yet, verses 18-24 compare and contrast the Christian journey to the Exodus from Egypt and the arrival at Mt. Sinai. In verse 22, followers of Christ are depicted as having reached symbolic Mt. Zion, "the city of the living God, the heavenly Jerusalem." This verse seems to contain both a present and a future orientation, especially in the light of verse 28. And the pilgrim motif occurs again in Hebrews 13:13, 14: Christians follow Jesus outside the gate and wait for the city to come.

But this motif is not limited to the last three chapters of Hebrews. We find it throughout the epistle. The introduction (1:3) portrays Jesus' procession into the heavenly sanctuary—which is the destination His disciples hope to reach. In chapters 3 and 4, God's people journey toward God's rest. Under Joshua, Israel entered Canaan, but they did not reach the real rest. Chapter 4:14-16 depicts Jesus as having "passed through the heavens," enabling His people to draw near the throne of grace. In chapter 9 we notice a movement from the earthly to the heavenly sanctuary. Jesus appears "in the presence of God for us" (9:24, NASB).

The idea of separation and the focus on the final destination are also prominent in Hebrews. Like Abraham, true Christians have left behind whatever may hinder them from serving the Lord completely and awaiting His kingdom. Nevertheless, the biblical concept of being a pilgrim and moving toward a goal in no way implies an effort to secure one's own salvation. Believers have already been saved though Christ's sacrifice. As their high priest, Jesus appears in God's presence for them.

Biblical pilgrims are not satisfied with this world and what it has to offer. They press toward the heavenly city—the heavenly sanctuary, the site where stands God's throne, the center of the universe, the place where they will enjoy a face-to-face relationship with the Lord. Because of this goal they faithfully follow their Lord by living in accordance with His will. They don't withdraw from the hustle and bustle of everyday life. But all the while they remember their higher calling, that of seeking the presence of the Lord. As wanderers between two worlds, their ethic is an interim ethic shaped by their focus on heaven.

II. Christians and Their Lord

Living as pilgrims poses challenges. Pilgrims do not constitute the majority. They may be considered weird and may face persecution. They may be tempted to give up their pilgrimage and settle down, to renounce their Lord and apostatize. "Whoever confuses his earthly home with salvation has lost the heavenly city, which God has prepared for the believers of all times."[4] Paul deals with this subject—apostasy—in three major blocks: Hebrews 6:4-6; 10:26-31; 12:15-17, 25-29. He doesn't tell the readers of Hebrews that some among them have already apostatized, but he says the danger of apostasy is always present. So he challenges them to follow Christ.

We can understand that Paul's concern drove him to try to motivate his readers to remain loyal to Jesus. Still, we find his statement in Hebrews 6:4-6 puzzling—that when those "who have tasted of the heavenly gift" fall away, "it is impossible to restore them again to repentance."

We best determine what the apostle is saying in this passage if we don't treat it in isolation, but study it instead in light of the two parallel passages. Johnsson has pointed out that the three blocks contain five common elements: (1) privileges, (2) offense, (3) result, (4) prospect of judgment, and (5) reasons for the divine rejection. Paul "describes acts of wanton rejection, of overt defiance of Jesus as Lord. [There's] no suggestion of a sin of omission or weakness. . . . Because Hebrews exalts the cross in such glowing terms, because it shows so emphatically its superlative worth, it must point out the horror of a deliberate rejection."[5]

Salvation is dependent on Jesus; "there is no other repentance than that provided by God through Jesus Christ."[6] If we reject Him deliberately, we've rejected salvation. So, the apostle encourages us to have a dynamic and vibrant relationship with the Lord, to have assurance, and to be steadfast in the faith.

III. Christians and Society

The assurance, the hope, and the promises believers have received through Christ's death and high-priestly ministry affect how they live, how they relate to God, and how they treat others. While the Epistle to the Hebrews deals with Christians' relationship to God, some verses seem also to be devoted to how they should relate to society.

First of all, as Jesus pointed out words in the Sermon on the Mount (Matt. 5:9), Christians should actively try to make peace. They oppose strife and war (12:14). By doing so, they serve their society and work toward its improvement. In addition, the apostle mentions hospitality that is not restricted to church members (13:2). Christians care for those at the margin of society—the outcasts, prisoners, and those ill-treated (13:3). Christians also care for those who suffer, those who are sick and desperate, those who have lost their belongings and their income (13:16). And Christians care for those who are doing fine and seem to need nothing.

Paul used the word *sacrifice* twice in Hebrews 13. While this word refers to the Old Testament sacrifices and to Jesus' sacrificial death, it has another dimension: Christians themselves also offer sacrifices. These sacrifices are not the means of salvation; rather, Christians offer them because they have already received salvation.[7] Since they've been blessed and are rich in Christ, they express their gratitude with sacrifices of praise to God (13:15) and deeds of mercy and service to their fellow human beings (13:16).[8]

"Sacrifices of praise, acts of kindness, and generosity together constitute the worship that God desires from the new covenant community in response to the experience of saving grace. Christians must glorify God not merely with their mouths but with their works as well."[9] The sanctuary language is still maintained. Even our practical life is related to the sanctuary.

Sacrifices in Hebrews

Sacrifices of the Old Testament System	
Abel's sacrifice	11:4
Sacrifices offered by priests	10:11
Sacrifices offered by the high priest	5:1; 7:27; 8:3
Sacrifices offered in the earthly sanctuary	9:8, 9; 10:1, 5, 8
Sacrifices of the New Covenant	
Sacrifices for heavenly things	9:23
Jesus as sacrifice	9:26; 10:12
No sacrifice beside that of Jesus	10:26
Spiritual sacrifices of believers	13:15, 16

Hebrews doesn't seem to emphasize evangelistic outreach, but it does not deny it either. So, it does not justify reducing our service to society to social action only. The biblical books complement each other.

IV. The Christian Community

The Christian church is like a family. The members form the "household of God," God's family (Eph. 2:19). Already in New Testament times Christians were calling one another "brother" and "sister." Family members take care of one another, encourage one another, and sometimes even confront one another to enhance growth and maturity (Heb. 10:24, 25). Unfortunately, we sometimes neglect this in our churches. Yet, such service can bless both the person helped and the helper.

Hebrews 10:19-25 takes what happened at the Cross and what is happening in heaven and connects it to our lives here and now and to our behavior as pilgrims.

Hebrews 10:19-25

- Because we have access to the sanctuary by Jesus' blood (19, 20)
- and because we have a high priest, (21)

1. Let us draw near with a sincere heart (22)
   - with hearts sprinkled clean and
   - bodies washed.

2. Let us hold fast the confession of our hope (23)

3. And let us consider how to stimulate one another to love and good works, (24)
   - not forsaking our meeting together, (25)
   - but encouraging one another.

Verses 19-21 lay out the prerequisite for what is discussed in the following verses. The emphasis is on Jesus, His cross, and His ministry as our high priest in heaven. As a result of what Jesus has done, we receive a threefold call and experience the privilege of salvation (10:22-25). This call affects our inner life, our relationship to God (10:22, 23), and our relationship to other Christians (10:24, 25).

Hebrews 10:19-25

1. *Prerequisites* (subordinate clause)	10:19-21
• Jesus' blood and sacrifice	10:19, 20
• Jesus' high-priestly ministry	10:21
2. *Consequences* (main clauses)	10:22-25
• Christians in their relationship to God (two imperatives and results)	10:22, 23
• Christians in their relationship to the Christian community (one direct imperative and two indirect imperatives)	10:24, 25

Whereas verse 25 speaks of encouraging one another, verse 24 contains an imperative that can be translated "consider," "think of," or—literally—"observe" one another for the encouragement of love and good works. In these days in which we are so oriented to individualism, we tend to forget our responsibility to our Christian brothers and sisters. At times we tend to withdraw from them, thinking that what they do and believe is their own business. But members of the Christian community need encouragement, appeals, and comfort—and regular fellowship in church meetings. Pilgrims must help fellow pilgrims.

No one should try to be a Christian in isolation unless circumstances force such a life. We need one another. Jesus created the church, and we need to get involved in it—to find friendships there, develop our gifts, and meet our Lord corporately. So, Paul challenges church members to see "that no one comes short of the grace of God; that no root of bitterness" springs up (12:15, NASB). They are to be motivated by brotherly love, to practice hospitality, and to care for the needy (13:1-3). They are to respect their leaders and pray for one another (13:7, 17, 18) while opposing false teachers (13:9).

V. The Christian Family and the Individual

The first part of Hebrews 13 deals with the Christian's relationship to fellow believers and to non-Christians. Into this context, Paul adds marriage relationships as well. The larger context is still the sanctuary.[10]

In Hebrews 13:4 the apostle stresses the importance and sanctity of marriage and warns against a misuse of sexual powers. In this text he differentiates between fornication and adultery—unless the Greek word "and" is understood as meaning "namely": "fornicators, namely adulterers." This is possible, but the way Scripture generally uses the word *fornication* makes it unlikely. Adulterers are married persons who maintain a sexual relationship with someone who is not their spouse. In this context, "fornicators" may refer to unmarried individuals who have sexual contact with married people.[11] Jesus said that sin starts with our thought processes (Matt. 5:27, 28). In our daily struggle for purity we need the help our High Priest can provide. "When the divine principles are recognized and obeyed in this relation, marriage is a blessing; it guards the purity and happiness of the race, it provides for man's social needs, it elevates the physical, the intellectual, and the moral nature."[12] Followers of Christ will treasure marriage and sexuality as they were designed by the Lord.

For many of us, money has a magical attraction. Lots of people worry about finances. And issues related to money comprise one of the most frequent causes of problems within marriages and families. Jesus Himself was once asked to intervene when two brothers fought over their inheritance. " 'Take care!' " He answered. " 'Be on your guard against all kinds of greed; for one's life does not consist in the abundance of possessions' " (Luke 12:15, NRSV). Then He told the parable of the rich fool.

Greed and the love of money destroy human relations. These vices ignore God and tempt people to think they don't need Him. In Hebrews 13:5 the apostle calls us to reject the love of money and to be content with what we have. Love of money or worries about our income reveal a lack of faith.[13] We would do well to heed these warnings, especially when we're tempted to measure the quality of life by what we do or do not have.

Followers of the Lord rely on God's wonderful promises, such as those found in Hebrews 13:5, 6. They trust in Jesus their Lord, who said, " 'Seek first His kingdom and His righteousness, and all these things shall be added to you' " (Matt. 6:33, NASB). We have been saved through Christ's sacrifice. Every day our Lord takes care of us. As pilgrims on the move to the heavenly city, we live—in accordance with God's will—a rich and abundant life.

Conclusion

The Christian walk is simultaneously difficult and easy: difficult because we have to "lay aside every . . . sin which so easily entangles us" and run the race with perseverance (12:1, NASB); easy because Jesus has saved us, has set the example, and empowers us to follow Him (13:21).

The anonymous letter to Diognetus, a piece of literature of early Christianity, says of Christians: "They dwell in their own fatherlands, but as if sojourners in them; they share all things as citizens, and suffer all things as strangers. Every foreign country is their fatherland, and every fatherland is a foreign country."[14]

The Christian life is an exodus or—to state it as Hebrews does, in a positive way—a joyous drawing near to the holy presence of God.[15]

---

1. See John 17:6-18.

2. See esp. Heb. 11:9-16; 12:1, 18-24; 13:13, 14. See also 1 Peter 1:1; 2:11.

3. The phrase "land of promise" is found in Heb. 11:9. This is the only place in Scripture where this phrase is found, although the concept is employed in many places.

4. Knut Backhaus, "Das Land der Verheißung: Die Heimat der Glaubenden im Hebräerbrief," *New Testament Studies* 47 (2001): 176 (translated).

5. Johnsson, *In Absolute Confidence,* 143, 145–148.

6. Ellingworth states: "Once Christ and his sacrifice have been rejected, there is nowhere else to turn" (323). See also Lane, *Hebrews 1–8,* 142. He goes on to say that in Hebrews "the apostate repudiates the only basis upon which repentance can be extended."

7. See Ellingworth, 722.

8. For an outline of this passage, see Lane, *Hebrews 9–13,* 503, 504.

9. Ibid., 549, 553.

10. See Heb. 13:10-15.

11. See F. F. Bruce, *The Epistle to the Hebrews, New International Commentary on the New Testament* (Grand Rapids: Wm. B. Eerdmans Publishing Co., 1970), 392; Ekkehardt Mueller, "Fornication," (Biblical Research Institute Webpage: biblicalresearch.gc.adventist.org, 2000), 7.

12. Ellen G. White, *The Adventist Home* (Nashville: Southern Publishing Association, 1952), 26.

13. See Jesus' statements in the Sermon on the Mount, Matt. 6:19-34.

14. *Diognetus* 5.5.

15. See Backhaus, 182.

CHAPTER 13

Jesus and Our Future

Most of us are interested in the future. We have to be, because we need to plan ahead. But we can't tell precisely what the future holds in stock for us. Many of those who have tried to predict the future have been spectacularly wrong:

- "Theoretically, television may be feasible, but I consider it an impossibility—a development which we should waste little time dreaming about."—*Lee de Forest, 1926, inventor of the cathode-ray tube*
- "I think there is a world market for about five computers."—*Thomas J. Watson, 1943, chairman of the board of IBM*
- "We don't think the Beatles will do anything in their market. Guitar groups are on their way out."—*Recording company expert, 1962*[1]

Do a search on the Internet for the term *future* and you'll find thousands of Web sites. You can read, for instance, about finance and the future, future harvest, space and the future, and resources for the future. You can even buy a CD by Holly Wynnette entitled *My Future Ex-Boyfriend!* And Web oracles offer their services discussing the threats of overpopulation; global warming; and intelligent, self-replicating machines that will replace humans. The scenarios range from life in a paradise to life as a nightmare.

Hebrews has a strong orientation toward the future, relating it to Jesus. He will return and usher in God's kingdom of glory. While Christians enjoy the privilege of being God's people here and now, they look forward to the final fulfillment of all promises—to the city of God and the time when they can see their Lord face to face.[2]

I. The Last Days

The very beginning of Hebrews contains an interesting clause: "In these last days [God] has spoken to us in His Son" (Heb. 1:2, NASB). Chapter 9:26 adds: "Now he has appeared once for all at the end of the ages to do away with sin by the sacrifice of himself" (NIV). The expressions "in these last days" and "at the end of the ages" refer to the time since the first coming of Christ. Obviously, the end time started with the first advent of our Savior. Scripture does not deny that there is a special end time before Jesus' return, but His first coming—including particularly His death and resurrection—was such a climactic event that it brought about a change of eras. The new age was superimposed on the old age.[3]

Other New Testament books contain statements similar to those found in Hebrews 1:2 and 9:26. According to 1 Corinthians 10:11, "the end of the ages has come." Jesus Himself described the new era with these words: " 'The kingdom of God is not coming with signs to be observed; nor will they say, "Look, here *it is!*" or, "There *it is!*" For behold, the kingdom of God is in your midst' " (Luke 17:20, 21, NASB). Peter wrote of Jesus appearing "in these last times" (1 Peter 1:20, NASB).

These phrases—"last days," "last times," "end of the ages," "the kingdom is in our midst," and others—do not deny the fact that it is Jesus' second coming that marks the ultimate end. After stating regarding Jesus' first advent that He "appeared once for all at the end of the age to put away sin by the sacrifice of himself" (Heb. 9:26), Paul went on to say: "so Christ, having been offered once to bear the sins of many, will appear a second time, not to deal with sin but to save those who are eagerly waiting for him" (vs. 28).

"With the first advent of Christ, the new age had broken into or overlapped the old. The two ages would continue to exist side by side until the Second Advent, when the old age would finally be destroyed."[4]

II. The Already and the Not Yet

In the New Testament, particularly in Paul's writings, we find the concept of the "already/not yet"—for example, we are already, yet not finally, saved.[5] Hebrews contains this concept. According to Hebrews 6:4, Christians "have [already] been enlightened and have tasted of the heavenly gift and have been made partakers of the Holy Spirit" (NASB) However, according to chapter 12:28, they will—future—receive an unshakable kingdom. According to Hebrews 2:8, God "left nothing that is not subject to him"—Jesus (NASB). But according to chapter 10:12, 13, Jesus "sat down at the right hand of God, then to wait until his enemies should be made a stool for his feet."

"Expressed in terms of time, the New Testament can describe the end as already present in one sense, yet future in another. The New Testament also expresses the same concept in terms of space—Christians live in heavenly places in Christ at the same time that they continue to struggle with the frustrations of this world. . . . A taste of the life of heaven begins immediately for everyone who believes in Jesus. . . . The difference between the now and the not-yet is not in the quality of the new age but in the fact that the old age is still present to distract and discourage."[6]

Those who don't hold both aspects of truth and accept them as complementary statements of the same reality become unbalanced and tend to move toward extreme positions that may end in heresy.

III. Future Events

The discussion on the last days and on the "already/not yet" shows that "when the New Testament is rightly understood, Jesus Christ is what the end is all about."[7] Hebrews presents the second coming of Jesus. Chapter 9 ends with the promise of His return. His incarnation, death, and high-priestly ministry prepare the way for His return. His followers "see the Day drawing near" (10:25), which motivates them to encourage one another and to attend the gatherings of the church. Quoting Habakkuk 2:3, 4, Paul said, "Yet a little while, and the coming one shall come and shall not tarry" (Heb. 10:37). He was referring to Jesus' second coming.[8]

The letter also points to events inseparably connected to Christ's return or events dependent on it. Speaking of "the resurrection of the dead," the author calls it "a better resurrection" (Heb. 6:2; 11:35, NASB). Hebrews confirms that bodily resurrections have happened in the past. However, there is another resurrection, which Jesus called the "resurrection of life" (John 5:29). It is linked to the Second Advent and brings immortality to God's children.

Hebrews contains several references to the future judgment, sometimes even connecting it to fire. Some believers today prefer to suppress the notions of a judgment and of God's wrath; they'd rather talk only about a loving and merciful God, a God without backbone. Preachers and others have misused the judgment when they've tried to make it the means of scaring people to repentance. But the fact that it has been misused is no excuse for ignoring what the Bible addresses.[9] Paul isn't afraid of warning people about God's judgment.

Hebrews speaks of the "eternal judgment" (6:2). It says death precedes it (9:27). God's adversaries expect this judgment with fear—"a fury of fire" will consume them (10:27). But God will judge His people (10:30) as well as fornicators and adulterers (13:4). Obviously, in most of these cases Paul was speaking about the executive judgment.

Fortunately, judgment has another side—namely, reward (Heb. 11:26) and final salvation (9:28). Moses' focus on the reward helped him to make right choices and to endure difficult circumstances. He directed his life toward that goal. Hebrews also connects judgment to "perfection" (11:40) and the heavenly fatherland, the city that is to come (11:16; 13:14). It notes that God will function as the judge (Heb. 12:23) and that He will reward His people.

Although Paul refers to Christ's second coming, the resurrection of the dead, and the judgment, he doesn't give the order of these events. Nor does he set up a timetable for them. Obviously, it is more important to live a holy life and thus to be ready whenever Jesus comes than to know precisely when certain events will happen.

Two other verses contain references to the future kingdom of God. Although believers have already tasted "the powers of the age to come" (Heb. 6:5), this "age" has not yet come. And Hebrews 12:14 (NASB) challenges Christians to "pursue peace . . . and the sanctification without which no one will see the Lord"—reminding us indirectly that we will see the Lord.

So, although the emphasis in Hebrews is on Christ's death and His high-priestly ministry in heaven, this book also has a clear focus on the Second Coming, the resurrection of the dead, the judgment, and the final reward.

IV. The Heavenly City

Three passages in Hebrews speak of the heavenly city: chapter 11:10-16; 12:18-24; and 13:12-14. The first passage (11:10-16) describes Abraham and the patriarchs. Abraham "had altogether different standards of value—a city whose foundations are utterly unshakeable. The writer thinks in spiritual terms of the city which God is building."[10] The patriarchs were pilgrims on the move to the real homeland, the heavenly fatherland, the city of God.

The second passage (12:18-24) describes the new covenant community. Whereas in the first passage Paul contrasts the tents and the earthly country with the heavenly city and homeland, in the second passage he contrasts Mount Sinai and Mount Zion. The southeastern hill of Jerusalem was called Mount Zion, which then became another name for the City of David and sometimes for the entire city of Jerusalem. When the ark of the covenant was brought into the city, and later, when Solomon built his temple, *Zion* became the name of the place where God dwelt.[11]

In our passage, Mount Zion seems to be synonymous with the terms "the city of the living God" and "the heavenly Jerusalem." It may describe the heavenly assembly and the invisible church, including the Godhead. In Hebrews 12:18-24, in the context of an "approving judgment," a festal gathering of angels and the people of God takes place in the immediate presence of the divine Judge. Believers are portrayed as having already come to the city of God.[12] We already belong to that heavenly city.

The third passage (Heb. 13:12-14) presents a contrast between the earthly Jerusalem, which Jesus was forced to leave, and the future city. The disciples follow Jesus "not only on the way to the cross here and now but ultimately to the final goal of the pilgrimage, the future heavenly city. There they will enjoy uninterrupted intimate fellowship with God."[13] Whereas the second passage says that Christ's disciples have already arrived at the heavenly city, the last passage reminds us that there is a future dimension and that they are still on the move to the consummation. They still have to persevere and should not fall away from Christ. Again the "already/not yet" is presented.

The city, which is our goal, is identical with the heavenly homeland, Mount Zion, the heavenly Jerusalem, the unshakable kingdom, the future city, and the heavenly sanctuary.[14] This city is the goal of all true pilgrims of all times. Our real home is not here on earth but in the presence of God; therefore, we do not live as if we have a permanent home here.[15]

V. The Sanctuary and the Second Coming

The book of Hebrews cannot be understood apart from the Old Testament sanctuary service. The substitutionary death of Christ for our sins and His high-priestly ministry make sense only in the context of the sacrificial system of the old covenant. Furthermore, the sanctuary is the dwelling place of God. When we talk about His throne and His reign, we are also talking about the heavenly temple. As the past and the present are linked to the sanctuary, so is the future—that is, Christ's second coming, including the accompanying and subsequent events. The entire plan of salvation is built around the concepts and symbols first revealed in the tabernacle on earth. In Christ, everything finds its fulfillment. There is no plan of salvation without the sanctuary!

Hebrews 9:24-28 connects the sanctuary setting to the sacrifice of Christ, His ministry in the heavenly sanctuary, and His second coming: (1) Through His sacrifice sin is put away (vss. 26, 28). (2) In heaven He "appear[s] in the presence of God for us" (vs. 24, NASB). (3) Salvation comes to full fruition only at His second coming (vs. 28). If the sanctuary points to salvation, and salvation is consummated in the Second Coming, then the sanctuary must be linked to the Second Coming.

Hebrews 10:11-13 contains the same sequence: (1) Jesus is the sacrifice, and sanctuary language is used of His death (vs. 12). (2) He "sat down at the right hand of God" (vs. 12). He is the Priest-King of Psalm 110. Furthermore, God's throne is found in the sanctuary. Thus, again the sanctuary is involved. (3) He "wait[s] until his enemies should be made a stool for his feet" (vs. 13). This is still future and has to do with His second coming and the final judgment of His enemies. Again the context is the sanctuary.

Hebrews 12:22-28 deals with the heavenly city. We hear about Christ's "sprinkled blood, which speaks better than the blood of Abel" (vs. 24, NASB), Jesus as the mediator of a new covenant (vs. 24), and then "a kingdom that cannot be shaken" that we will receive (vs. 28). Clearly, the sanctuary is involved in all three phases.

Thus, Hebrews links the sanctuary with the second coming of Christ. The teaching about the sanctuary and the teaching about the last things belong together and should not be separated.

Conclusion

God's children are "on the march. Although already consecrated and separated, they seek the center of the universe, the very (actually realized) presence of God."[16] Hebrews 9:28 stresses this longing and seeking by saying that Christians "eagerly await him"—Jesus, their Sacrifice, High-Priestly Mediator, and King.

We concentrate on our Lord. We expect Him to come soon and can hardly wait for His second advent. This goal shapes our life. We are on the way to seeing God face to face!

---

1. See <http://www.christianglobe.com/Illustrations/>.
2. The word *hope* is found five times in the book (Heb. 3:6; 6:11, 18; 7:19; 10:23) and emphasizes how important it is to live with a clear goal.

3. See Guthrie, 63, and Ellingworth, 93.

4. Jon Paulien, *What the Bible Says About the End-Time* (Hagerstown: Review and Herald, 1994), 77, 78.

5. According to Eph. 2:4-6, Christians "have been saved"; but according to Rom. 8:23, we are "waiting eagerly for . . . the redemption of our body" (NASB). See also John 5:24; Matt. 19:29.

6. Paulien, 77, 79.

7. Ibid., 81.

8. The Hebrew text talks about the fulfillment of the vision. In the Septuagint there's a shift from the vision to a person. Hebrews clearly understands it as a Messianic prophecy applying to Christ' return. For a discussion, see Bruce, 272–274.

9. See Acts 20:20, 27.

10. Guthrie, 232.

11. Cp., Siegfried Horn, *Seventh-day Adventist Bible Dictionary,* 791213.

12. See Lane, *Hebrews 9–13,* 470, 466.

13. Ibid., 547.

14. Johnsson, *In Absolute Confidence,* 154, notes that God's city "is the place par excellence."

15. See Ellen G. White, *Testimonies for the Church* (Nampa, Idaho: Pacific Press Publishing Association, 1948), 9:287, 288.

16. Johnsson, *In Absolute Confidence,* 155.